It has been a privilege to know Ken Hemphill and his passion for in-depth study of God's Word. His new book *Making Change* will be a great help to see how we can tap into God's resources as we seek to accomplish the Great Commission.

—Johnny Hunt, Pastor
First Baptist Church, Woodstock, Georgia

If there was ever a time for biblical and kingdom perspective on finances, it is today. And if there ever was a man who was best equipped to give this kingdom perspective, it is Ken Hemphill. Prepare to dig deeply into God's Word. Prepare to be challenged. And, if you are listening carefully, prepare to be changed. What a great contribution to the biblical understanding of stewardship.

—Thom S. Rainer, President and CEO
LifeWay Christian Resources

Dr. Ken Hemphill continues to challenge Southern Baptists to be a kingdom people. His numerous books, articles, and studies are helping churches and individuals to focus on God's glory and lordship. No where is God's kingdom reign more apparent than in the area of stewardship and finances. Hemphill's new book *Making Change* will be a practical and valuable tool to guide us in submitting to Christ the use of our income and material assets for the sake of His kingdom.

—Jerry Rankin, President
International Mission Board, SBC

In today's high pressured world, a sometimes overwhelming pressure point is finances! How do we get them, keep them, and wisely spend them? This is often quoted as the number one tension point in families and singles. *Making Change* doesn't lecture us, but wisely leads us to discover how to maximize life while minimizing the pressure. If you want to enjoy the ride a bit more, pick this up for the trip!

—Bob Reccord, President
North American Mission Board

Once again, Dr. Hemphill challenges us with the deep truths of the kingdom. In this wonderful book *Making Change* we discover the biblical principles and the theological foundation for financial matters in the life of Christ's followers. *Making Change* teaches us the fundamental truth that everything belongs to God, and we are His appointed stewards of the possessions that He has put into our care, so we might fulfill His purpose and bring Him glory. Written with careful scholarship and practical application for everyday living, *Making Change* will set Christ's followers and His church on glorious path to honor the King!

—Eric J. Thomas, Senior Pastor
First Baptist Church, Norfolk, Virginia

MAKING
CHANGE

A Transformational Guide to
Christian Money Management

KEN HEMPHILL

BROADMAN
& HOLMAN
PUBLISHERS

Nashville, Tennessee

Ten-digit ISBN: 0-8054-4426-2
Thirteen-digit ISBN: 978-0-8054-4426-1

Published by Broadman & Holman Publishers,
Nashville, Tennessee

Dewey Decimal Classification: 248.6
Subject Heading: STEWARDSHIP \ PERSONAL FINANCE

All Scripture is from the Holman Christian Bible® Copyright © 1999,
2000, 2002, 2003 by Holman Bible Publishers. Used by permission.

1 2 3 4 5 6 7 8   10 09 08 07 06

Contents

Foreword

by Morris H. Chapman

Making Change has the potential to lead you to a rewarding new life unburdened by our culture's obsession with credit cards and oversized mortgages. The topic of stewardship is one of the most overlooked and under-utilized teachings in the Bible. Consequently, we are living in a generation that owes its soul to company stores and financial institutions.

The Bible shows us the way through the wilderness of an over-indulgent lifestyle that leads to ever-mounting debt. Though surprising to many, God's Word is peppered throughout with extraordinarily profound counsel about sound money management. In fact, the financial wisdom found in the Word of God is far greater than what is found in *Fortune, Forbes, Money Magazine,* and the *Wall Street Journal* combined or taught at Harvard and Wharton business schools. The Scriptures offer a wealth of advice on how to honor God by the way we make money, spend money, give money, save money, invest money, and leave money for our families.

Unfortunately, biblical stewardship and wise money management seem to be lost disciplines in contemporary Christian life. Americans spend $1.20 for every dollar they earn and have $600 billion in credit card debt, averaging nearly $8,300 per family. Many families have as many as three or four credit cards. Some even use one credit card simply to pay the interest on the others. In fact, about 14 percent of a family's expendable income is used to pay the interest on credit card debt. Consequently, Americans are only saving at a level of about 2.2 percent, and it should come as no surprise that giving through the local church is at an all-time low of 2.6 percent.

The results are telling and even tragic. Personal finances are over-extended, bank accounts are overdrawn, families are overcome with debt, and sadly many marriages are just plain *over*. Financial problems are one of the primary reasons cited in divorce cases. Moreover, people are living longer and their inadequate savings are running out. Finally, money for missions and ministry is declining at a time when we are blessed with an unprecedented opportunity to spread the gospel. We have forgotten the essential biblical principles on how to honor God by the way we manage the financial resources he has entrusted to us.

Like most things, the failure in large part is a failure of leadership. Far too long church leaders have listened to the so-called church growth gurus who told us that we shouldn't talk about money. At the same time, we have mostly ignored the strong emphasis placed on money management in the Old Testament writings, the prominence placed on stewardship in Jesus' teachings, and the tremendous kingdom impact of cooperative giving in the mission efforts of the New Testament church.

The Old Testament contains solid stewardship principles. Consider the fact that the first chapter of the first book of the Bible begins with God—God is the Creator and therefore the owner of everything. When God made mankind, He entrusted us as the managers and stewards of earth's resources. As we read further, we find the principles of giving God our offering and his tithe in recognition of his ownership and as an expression of our dependence and gratitude. The book of Proverbs is literally packed with practical wisdom on how to make money, spend money, save money, and invest money.

In the New Testament, we find that the Lord Jesus had much to say about money management and possessions. Conservative estimates are that 15 percent of Jesus' teachings focused on finances. For example, Jesus says that if we can be trusted in our stewardship of material things (the lesser), He will give us stewardship over spiritual things (the greater). The opposite is also true (Luke 16:10-12). The way we handle material possessions on earth is a good test of what we would do with responsibilities in the kingdom of heaven.

Jesus also teaches that the way we view, value, and handle money is a key indicator of the desire of our hearts: "Where your treasure is, there your heart will be also" (Matt. 6:21). He points out that hoarding up earthly treasures is futile; investing in heavenly treasure yields benefits both now and for eternity.

Did you know that the day is going to come when all we are going to have is what we have given to God? This is why God wants us to invest in his kingdom and the souls of men, the only permanent things that exist. Think about it. Dew drops are as pretty as diamonds, but when the sun rises, they disappear. Most people are making investments in things that are going to evaporate like dew drops in the heat of the sun.

In fact, Jesus affirms that "heaven and earth will pass away" (Matt. 24:35). Further, the Bible teaches that the world will be consumed with fire (2 Pet. 3:10–12). Consider this: Everything we are slaving to buy and slaving to keep, God says is going up in smoke! Again, only the kingdom and the souls that will populate eternity are permanent, so that is where we need to invest.

What is the rate of return on investing in the kingdom and its causes? Jesus said it is 10,000 percent! No, that is not a misprint. The return on investment (R.O.I.) is 10,000 percent. How many have stocks or mutual funds that are paying 10,000 percent? It is safe to say that no one has that good of an R.O.I. Yet Jesus said: "Everyone who has left houses, brothers or sisters, father or mother, children, or fields because of My name will receive 100 times more and will inherit eternal life" (Matt. 19:29).

Get out a calculator, run the numbers, and you will find that one-fold is a 100 percent gain and one hundred fold actually means a gain of 10,000 percent. That makes the kingdom of God the best investment we could ever make, and it benefits us on both sides of death. By investing in eternity while we are still on Earth, we live out a kingdom principle best expressed by Pastor Adrian Rogers: "You can't take it with you, but you can send it on ahead by investing in the only thing going to heaven, and that is the souls of men."

When we read further into the pages of the New Testament, we find the apostle Paul calling on churches to give offerings for ministry and missions. He challenged Christians to give as God prospered them, to give systematically on the first day of the week, to give sacrificially and joyously, and to give corporately for kingdom causes. The churches responded by cooperating in their giving so that Paul and others could go and that together they could reach their world for Christ and His kingdom.

Southern Baptists seek to follow this New Testament model. Missions and evangelism are our heartbeat, so we not only encourage personal soul-winning, but we also have a unique plan for pooling our collective financial resources and strategically distributing them to reach the world with the gospel. We call this tremendous ministry tool the Cooperative Program. Established in 1925, the Cooperative Program remains the most efficient and effective funding method for accomplishing the Acts 1:8 mandate to be Christ's witnesses—beginning where we are and ultimately reaching to the ends of the earth. Since no one individual or single church can fully realize this biblical mandate alone, our predecessors wisely decided that we can do far more together.

Because of the faithful giving of Southern Baptists, we are able to launch disaster relief teams to places of desperate need, dispatch medical missionaries to AIDS ravaged Africa, repair inner-city homes all across America, offer hope to hardened hearts in our nation's prisons, speak on behalf of righteousness in the halls of government, train, equip, and send out armies of pastors, chaplains, ministers, and missionaries, start 63 new churches every day, and baptize 1 person every 37 seconds. The Cooperative Program enables Southern Baptist givers to participate in all of this, and much, much more. Yet everything we do has the same goal, aim, and mission—to show and share the love of Jesus Christ with every person in every part of the world.

Consequently I would not only encourage all Southern Baptists to take pride in what we are able to accomplish through the Cooperative Program, but also challenge each of us to feel a renewed sense of urgency to give systematically and sacrificially so that together we might do more than ever before to obey the Great Commission of our Lord. Indeed, what I believe to be the greatest missionary enterprise since the book of Acts ultimately depends on the individual who is faithful to pray, faithful to witness, and faithful to give.

Have you ever considered the fact that your biblical stewardship may be the specific witness that leads someone to Christ? Some years ago, Dr. Vander Warner, former pastor of Grove Avenue Baptist Church in Richmond, Virginia, and past president of the Southern Baptist pastors' conference, told of a beautiful young woman and handsome young man in his church who were engaged to be married. One evening they got together to work on their wedding plans, and afterward, she drove home.

Tragically, on a rain-slick street in Richmond, there was the crash of metal and the breaking of glass, and she was killed in the accident. When the police arrived on the scene and went through her effects to identify her, the only number they could find was her fiancé's. They called him, identified him, described what had happened, and he rushed to the scene of the accident. With great sadness, he identified his beloved fiancé with whom he'd spent that evening, planning for the years to come.

However, as the heartbroken young man was about to leave, a policeman came up and asked him: "What kind of young lady was this?" The young man said: "What do you mean?" The officer puzzled: "The only other thing we found in her car was a bank statement, and canceled checks. We were trying to find some way to identify her, and we found check after check written out to: Grove Avenue Baptist Church, Grove Avenue Baptist Church, Grove Avenue Baptist Church . . . What was she?"

The broken young man gathered himself enough to explain why so many checks were written to Grove Avenue Baptist Church. Then, standing by the wreckage that claimed the life of his bride to be, the young man led the officer to saving faith in the Lord Jesus Christ. What would your canceled checks tell a lost man about your relationship to Jesus Christ? Your obedience to biblical stewardship could become the witness that helps lead someone to Christ.

We need to return to the basic principles of stewardship and money management found in God's word. That's why I am excited about the potential of this powerful new resource written by Ken Hemphill entitled *Making Change: A Transformational Guide to Christian Money Management*. Ken has done a masterful job mining treasure from the Scriptures in this 30-day journey into money management from a kingdom perspective. In these pages, I hope you will rediscover God's kingdom plan for the material resources he has entrusted to us as his children.

Ken Hemphill has become a warrior for the Kingdom as he travels about the country from church to church, association to association, and state convention to state convention challenging Southern Baptists to be a kingdom people. The Southern Baptist Convention adopted a convention-wide vision entitled *Empowering Kingdom Growth* (EKG) based upon Matthew 6:3 "Seek ye first the kingdom of God, and his righteousness; and all these things shall be added unto you."

The Mission Statement of *EKG* states that "Empowering Kingdom Growth is an initiative designed to call individual Southern Baptists to renew their passion for the Lord Jesus and the reign of His Kingdom in their hearts, families, and churches from which God can forge a spiritual movement marked by holy living, sacrificial service, and global witness."

Ken Hemphill came to the SBC position of strategist for Empowering Kingdom Growth from the presidency of Southwestern Baptist Theological Seminary and has devoted himself, his time, and his energy to the task of taking the vision of EKG to the people called Southern Baptists. Thousands of churches have engaged in the 40-day study written by Ken entitled, *The Heartbeat of God*. This exciting study already has revitalized individual Christians, thereby bringing a new vision to many of our churches that is focused upon putting God first in our lives and generating a renewed enthusiasm for the kingdom of God. As you study this book, I urge you to pray that God will transform the EKG vision into a powerful movement of God's Holy Spirit upon and among His people that shall lead to a mighty spiritual awakening in our nation and beyond.

A second multi-week study has been incorporated into the EKG family entitled, *Acts 1:8,* authored by Nate Adams. In this book, Nate identifies the biblical strategy for reaching the world for Christ, a strategy Jesus gave the church and to which he calls every Christian in every church to engage for the kingdom's sake.

Making Change is the third study offered as a part of the *Empowering Kingdom Growth* vision. It is a journey through the maze of biblical stewardship, personal money management, and cooperative giving for the purposes of world missions and theological education.

If Southern Baptists are to expand their missions force in the world, practicing biblical stewardship is absolutely critical. Not until a kingdom-minded people, employing a kingdom-minded missions strategy, and obeying the kingdom-minded principles of biblical stewardship, will God's people ever reach deeply into the spiritual darkness that exists on every continent on Earth including our own.

Making Change will teach you how and why to rise above financial challenges and victoriously *transform* you into a person whose faithful stewardship will add incalculable value to your life and the possibility of helping others with the greatest transformation of all, trusting Christ as personal Savior. What greater value can be added to a person's life than the assurance that heaven will be home forever?

PREFACE

This book was birthed in the heart of Dr. Morris Chapman, president of the Executive Committee of the Southern Baptist Convention. Morris has a passion to see local churches and their mission partners—the convention entities—prosper with the goal of fulfilling the Acts 1:8 commandment. His passion for the kingdom has caused him to ask how we might strengthen the historic partnerships we have in place for cooperative ministry. It became obvious that a new tool was needed to teach the basics of Scripture as they relate to the funding of a mission enterprise that partners with local churches to reach the ends of the earth with the gospel. We must be both honest and candid—we are not committed to reaching the world until we are willing to allow God to provide the resources through us.

This book was first an assignment and then a labor of love and conviction. As I studied the classic texts dealing with money, God began to develop in my heart a passion for this book and the accompanying 40-day study. It is my prayer and conviction that God may use this book to bring spiritual awakening in our day. As I read again the book of Malachi, I was stunned to hear the prophet tell people that the conditions of apathy that were plaguing Israel were the direct result of robbing God of tithes and offerings. The key to revival, he declared, was rectifying this situation. If and when we experience revival, the issue of our stewardship will have already been resolved and the reaching of the nations will become practical reality.

Every book is actually a team project, and this one certainly fits in that category. I want to thank my colleagues in the Executive Committee building for their encouragement and help with this bold undertaking. I am particularly indebted to Morris Chapman, who gave me the assignment and the freedom to accomplish the task. Mary Creson, my assistant, has been invaluable in keeping the Empowering Kingdom Growth ministries functioning during those times when I am deeply committed to writing projects like this one.

I have considered the content of this book to be so important to the kingdom task before us that I have asked several people to read behind me and to give me critical input. I thank my pastor, Glenn Weekly, who was willing to read even while homebound recovering from surgery. My former assistant at Southwestern, Barbara Walker, has once again volunteered her time to suggest stylistic changes. Dr. Berry Driver has provided invaluable assistance in reading the manuscript for exegetical, theological, and historical accuracy.

I have been privileged to work with LifeWay Christian Resources and its publishing division, Broadman & Holman, in the publication of numerous books designed to encourage the local church. Ken Stephens and his entire team have demonstrated great enthusiasm for this project. In truth, they have gone beyond their normal good service to fast-track this book, ensuring that it would be available quickly to provide a follow-up study to *Empowering Kingdom Growth*. These two resources are unique in that the trade book is a B&H product and the 40-day study is a LifeWay product. Sam House, on the LifeWay side, has exhibited enthusiasm and manifested a servant spirit throughout the development of the product line.

I cannot adequately thank Lawrence Kimbrough, who is far more than an editor. He is a rewriter. His ability to take the drafts I give him and make them come alive is a gift. Lawrence is truly a kingdom-focused man. He is a great writer himself, and yet he willingly provides assistance to others who feel led to provide written materials to assist believers and their churches.

Paula, my companion of thirty-seven years, continues to be my writing partner. She not only listens to me as I read the rough drafts aloud to her, but she provides significant insights that always shape the materials I am writing. My girls and their husbands remain a constant source of pleasure and inspiration as they serve God in their given contexts. My two oldest daughters have provided for us two bundles of kingdom joy—Lois and Emerson, our first two granddaughters. You will find that stories of my family are scattered throughout the book. Thank you Brett, Kristina, and Lois Boesch; Trey, Rachael, and Emerson Oswald; and Daniel and Katie Banks for being yourselves.

Week 1, Day 1

The King and His Creation

In the beginning God created the heavens and the earth.

GENESIS 1:1

The earth and everything in it, the world and its inhabitants, belong to the Lord; for He laid its foundation on the seas and established it on the rivers.

PSALM 24:1–2

When you read the first words of the Bible—"In the beginning"—what goes through your mind? Do you think the phrase is nothing more than an obvious starting point with little more relevance than the introductory phrase from a good fairy tale—"Once upon a time"?

I'm afraid we sometimes do read it that way—so quickly and casually that we overlook its fundamental significance. But why do you think the Bible begins in this manner?

It is quite true (and patently obvious) that "in the beginning" does indeed declare the inauguration of everything. But it is much more than a marking of time! Eighteen other times when this Hebrew word is used in the Bible, it's translated this precise way: "In the beginning." But it can also be translated as "choice" or "firstfruits."[1] In other words, it is appropriate to say that creation is God's gift to himself—the "choice," the "firstfruits" of his divine activity.

But this interpretation of these powerfully familiar words only scratches the surface of the deep truths imbedded inside—truths that have much to say to us about every aspect of our lives.

Even our perspectives on stewardship.

In the Beginning

1. *"In the beginning" means there was more to come.*

Implicit in this assertion is the fact that God himself was the one directing what that "more" would be. When we witness the days of creation through the perspective of Genesis 1—the heavens, the earth, the sky, the seas, the plants, the starry hosts, the animal kingdom, and ultimately man— we realize that these were all created with intentionality and purpose by one who existed before anything was. All things were created by him!

If being part of God's deliberate act of creation is not sufficient in itself to take our breath in sheer wonder, we are further awed by this additional understanding: we were not only created purposefully but personally. God created us by himself and for himself, and he remains involved in our lives even today. He desires us to live in relationship with him and to join him in his purposeful activity.

2. *"In the beginning" also anticipates its ultimate end.*

Kenneth Mathews writes, "'Beginning' is often paired in the Old Testament with its antonym 'end,' indicating an inclusive period of time.[2] Isaiah the prophet certainly bore this out, recording the Lord's words this way: "Remember what happened long ago, for I am God, and there is no other; . . . I declare the end from the beginning, and from long ago what is not yet done, saying, My plan will take place and I will do all My will" (Isa. 46:9–11).

Thus, "in the beginning" declares that the creation of the heavens and the earth were initiated with a future goal in mind. They have meaning. They are going somewhere. God, the sovereign Creator, controls both the beginning and the end, moving everything toward his ultimate kingdom purpose—the centrality of Christ, the firstborn over all creation.

Paul spoke to this issue with startling clarity in his letter to the Colossians, declaring of Christ that everything was created by him, through him, and for him. He was not a part of the created order but existed before it and holds all of it together.

At this juncture we are startled by Paul's further pronouncement—that Christ is also "the head of the body, the church; He is the beginning, the firstborn from the dead, so that He might come to have first place in every-thing" (Col. 1:18). God's ultimate purpose is to reconcile everything to himself—things on earth and things in heaven. And he will do this through Christ, through his body known as the church, a covenant community of believers who are even now a key part of that divine plan.

3. *"In the beginning" means that the Creator is also the owner.*

This truth perhaps has the greatest bearing on our everyday lives and our attitudes toward nature, money, and material things. God is the owner and king of everything by virtue of the fact that everything was created by him and for him. Whenever the word *create* is used in the Old Testament, it speaks of divine activity. It means "to originate, to bring into being some-thing distinctively new out of nothing."

Therefore, the subject of creation is always God; all the rest are only direct objects. This is crucial to our understanding of who we are and how we relate both to God and to his created order.

Creator as Owner

To understand this better, we need to look at creation not merely as a Genesis event but as a theme throughout Scripture.

The creation narrative, you probably know, is written in two parts that are complementary, not contradictory. The first section (1:1–2:3) is focused on God; the second (2:4–24) is focused toward man and the earth. The first stresses the sovereign power of God; the second declares that the chief pur-pose of creation is the joy of communion between the Creator and man, the crown of God's creation.

But the word *created* is not confined to the book of Genesis. It so perme-ates the Bible that it is found dotted throughout the Scripture—twenty times alone in chapters 40–66 of Isaiah. If you read that section, you will discover that the prophet was intent on distinguishing between Israel's God as the true Lord of history—its Creator—in contrast to the Babylonian practices of idolatry and astrology.

But the language of creation is not limited to the Old Testament either. The writer of Hebrews declared: "By faith we understand that the universe was created by the word of God, so that what is seen has been made from things that are not visible" (Heb. 11:3).

John, in his Gospel, gives us a glimpse at the time before creation: "In the beginning was the Word, and the Word was with God, and the Word was God. He was with God in the beginning. All things were created through

Him, and apart from Him not one thing was created that has been created" (John 1:1–3).

Truly, the doctrine of creation appears everywhere in the Bible, and it yields some profound implications.

Foremost is the truth that *the Creator has the right and responsibility to ensure that his creation serves his purposes.* This theme is a virtual refrain of the psalmist: "The earth and everything in it, the world and its inhabitants belong to the LORD" (Ps. 24:1).

God himself spoke of this in referring to the offerings that were being brought before him, noting: "For every animal of the forest is Mine, the cattle on a thousand hills. I know every bird of the mountains and the creatures of the field are Mine" (Ps. 50:10–11).

Therefore, *God's creation should motivate in us a response of worship.* This is dictated by the understanding that the Creator is both owner and king. "For the LORD is a great God, a great King above all gods. The depths of the earth are in His hand, and the mountain peaks are His. The sea is His; He made it. His hands formed the dry land. Come, let us worship and bow down; let us kneel before the LORD our Maker" (Ps. 95:3–6).

This also means that we depend on him for everything. Through the prophet Isaiah the Lord declares: "Heaven is My throne, and earth is My footstool. . . . My hand made all these things, and so they all came into being" (Isa. 66:1a, 2a).

When the Lord answered the long-suffering Job, he pointed him back to creation. "Where were you when I established the earth? Tell me, if you have understanding. Who fixed its dimensions? Certainly you know! Who stretched a measuring line across it? Who supports its foundations? Or who laid its cornerstone?" (Job 38:4–6). The bottom line of God's response to Job was this: "Everything under heaven belongs to Me" (Job 41:11b). And we, like our brother Job of an earlier era, remain accountable to our Creator and dependent on him for every single thing we need.

Owner and Manager

The Jews were instructed to let their fields lie fallow every seven years. But this forerunner to crop rotation had a far more significant purpose than simply renewing the land. For after seven cycles of Sabbath years— every fiftieth year—a year of Jubilee was to be celebrated. This year of Jubilee provided rest for the soil, provision for the poor, and the restoration of the land back to the original owner.

Some of these ideas seem foreign to our ears, but they were based on a fundamental premise: "The land is not to be permanently sold because it is Mine, and you are only foreigners and temporary residents on My land" (Lev. 25:23).

God is the owner; man is the manager.

Perhaps it is unnecessary to state the obvious, but it seems not to have occurred to many of us: *if God is the Creator and owner, then we are not!*

"What do you *mean* I'm not the owner? I have a deed to my house! I own a car, stocks, bonds, clothes. I own *lots* of stuff!"

But let me tell you what else we own when we operate from that mindset. We own the stress in life that keeps us from being kingdom-focused people. When we think we own something, we feel duty bound to protect it. We have a tendency to hoard it and hide it to keep someone else from taking it away from us. Playing the role of owner comes with all kinds of unseen, unadvertised headaches.

But listen to this: if you want to discover true liberation, stress-free living, and exciting purpose in your life, banish from your vocabulary the idea of *ownership* and replace it with one of *stewardship*. God is the owner; we are the stewards. Therefore, if we want to succeed in life, we will manage his resources according to his design and desire.

We'll return to this profound idea throughout this study, but I want you to think personally about the implications of this truth.

How would your life change if you agreed with God's Word about this fundamental truth of creation—that everything belongs to the Creator and was designed by him to serve his kingdom purpose?

Take a moment to reflect on this. Write down some of the first things that come to mind.

A couple I was once privileged to pastor took God's ownership so seriously that they had a family ceremony where they literally, officially deeded everything over to God. But not long after this event, the washing machine malfunctioned. The husband told me that in the past this event would have produced great stress for them. In this instance, however—operating from a whole new, biblical standpoint—they laughed when it dawned on them that it wasn't *their* appliance that was broken; it was God's! They actually knelt and prayed, saying, "Lord, your washing machine has quit working. What do you want us to do about it?"

Whether you have an official ceremony to acknowledge God's ownership over all your possessions doesn't alter the fact that he *is* the owner. We are merely the managers.

God Is the Subject

God is the subject of the first sentence of the Bible. "In the beginning, God." He is also the subject of all that comes thereafter. And herein lies one of man's fundamental problems, which ultimately and inevitably leads us into rebellion—

We think *we* are the subject of the sentence.

We think life revolves around us! This creates a condition I call "spiritual my-opia," where we see everything from the perspective of "me" and "mine," always asking the frontline question, "What's in this for me?"

Don't think for a second, though, that this question is only on the lips of secular man. We hear of Christians looking for a church that meets "my needs." We play games with our spouse because he or she doesn't meet our emotional needs. We pray simple little prayers focused almost entirely on ourselves, even though the Father has assured us that he knows our needs before we do (Matt. 6:8).

"Spiritual my-opia" is pandemic, and there is only one cure: *we must let God be the subject of our lives.*

The recounting of Earth's creation in the early part of Genesis is dominated by a singular word—God. The first section is accentuated by the exclusive name *Elohim*, which occurs thirty-four times in thirty-four verses, dominating the whole chapter and catching our eye at every point on the page. It is a name that signifies his absolute, unqualified power and majesty.

Beginning in Genesis 2:4, however, the covenant name *Yahweh* begins to appear in conjunction with Elohim. Yahweh is more frequently used when the focus is on God's covenant relationship with his people. Thus, it is understandable that this name would be used when the emphasis of the narrative turns toward the creation of man, who is designed to live in covenant relationship with his Creator.

But no matter where you turn, the subject is God! The activity is creation! And the implications are staggering to contemplate!

Everything on earth was created by him and for him. *We* were created by him and for him. The sovereign God of the universe desires that we know him in intimate relationship and join him in kingdom activity.

Therefore, only when we rightly understand the context of his ownership can our lives have meaning and purpose. We can only know true happiness when we accept and act upon the principles of stewardship he designed into creation.

It Was Very Good

God saw all that He had made, and it was very good.
GENESIS 1:31A

Recently we were blessed with two beautiful granddaughters. I'll never forget the celebration of their first birthdays. My daughters and their husbands are much more enlightened parents than my wife and I were twenty-some years ago. They had been raising our grandbabies by the book. Case in point— neither of our grandchildren had tasted sweets until their first birthday.

Lois was the first to celebrate, and after an uncertain first taste of a beautiful chocolate cake, she dove in with unbridled enthusiasm. About six weeks later it was Emerson's turn to partake. Her mom picked a bit of the frosting off and placed it in Emerson's mouth, who began daintily to pick at the colorful splotches of icing, shoving them in her mouth and offering them on her fingers to her mom. She wanted to share this taste sensation with others.

Both Lois and Emerson had discovered that cake was *very good!*

As we read the book of Genesis, we are awed by the truth that the triune God created Earth for his glory and man's habitation and that he simply spoke it into existence by the authority of his word. The majesty and power of his act is overwhelming.

But lest we lose ourselves entirely in spiritual wonder, God left us with this report on the status of his earthly creation:

It was good. It was very good.

The Sevenfold Declaration

In the first chapter of Genesis alone, we find seven distinct pronouncements of the goodness of the created order (vv. 4, 10, 12, 18, 21, 25, 31). In the first instance God declared the *light* good because it dispelled the darkness that had once characterized the earth. In the second instance God declared the *vegetation* good, seeing it burst into bloom and covering the earth with beauty. And on and on and on.

God was systematically preparing the world for life's myriad possibilities and for man's habitation. And at each point he could stand back and affirm that it was good. As one writer describes God's assessment of his creative genius, "If the details of His work were pronounced 'good,' the whole is *very good.*"[3]

The Bible teaches that all created things were derived from God. Therefore, they are good simply because they reflect his character and declare his glory.

But there is more. To say that they are good indicates that the Creator has assigned to everything value and meaning. This is a critical matter. When God declared everything good, it indicated that he was the sole judge who could evaluate the consequences of his own creative activity and the subsequent use of his resources.

There is worth in creation—and in you—simply because God says so.

The Bible throughout affirms the goodness of God's world. Its bounty is designed not only to meet our needs but to bring joy to our hearts. The psalmist declared: "He causes grass to grow for the livestock and provides crops for man to cultivate, producing good from the earth, wine that makes man's heart glad—making his face shine with oil—bread that sustains man's heart" (Ps. 104:14–15). The writer of Ecclesiastes joins the refrain: "I know that there is nothing better for them than to rejoice and enjoy the good life. It also is the gift of God whenever anyone eats, drinks, and enjoys all his efforts" (Eccl. 3:12–13).

Good or Bad?

This biblical view of material things offers quite a contrast to that of other worldviews. Many of the pagan creation myths from early time periods depicted matter as threatening and sinister. Gnosticism, a heresy that developed early in the first century, taught that the world was inherently evil. Such a view of material things easily led to legalistic asceticism, a lifestyle clearly inconsistent with the teaching of Scripture.

In 1 Timothy 4, Paul countered such a worldview by pointing to the goodness of God's creation. He decried the attitudes and activities of those who "forbid marriage and demand abstinence from foods that God created to be received with gratitude by those who believe and know the truth. For everything created by God is good, and nothing should be rejected if it is received with thanksgiving" (vv. 3–4).

This is key: recognizing that the material creation of God has both a source and a purpose bears significant impact on our worldview, and consequently on how we live.

For example, the followers of Hinduism view the world as temporary and worthless, as unreal and illusory. Visit a Hindu nation, and you will observe firsthand the impact of such a worldview.

Buddhists want to do away with all desire. This is why they practice an eightfold path they hope will lead them to a passionless peace called *nirvana*. Material things are frowned upon because they contribute to man's desires.

But there is also an aberration of these, as practiced by those who see material things as being of the *greatest* value. Leo Garrett argues that both Marxism and unbridled capitalism, while arch foes in many respects, stand on common ground when they ascribe to material things the highest value known to living man.[4] When life's value is measured in terms of material possessions, one's relationship with God and others always become secondary.

The biblical view offers a profound corrective to all these misunderstandings when seen as the precise balance of two concepts that almost seem to be in conflict, at least in practical terms.

1. *All material things were created by and derived from God.* They are for this reason good. They have value, worth, meaning, and purpose.

2. *Yet they are temporal and not eternal.* Therefore, the Christian can never view material things as the ultimate reality. Despite popular thinking, the winner is not the one who dies with the most stuff. The use of material things must be consistent with our created purpose—a reality that is filled with true, genuine meaning yet is larger and much more far-reaching than our present experience.

The Appropriate Use of Created Things

I was sitting by the window one day as our plane began its descent into Alaska, overwhelmed by the beauty and majesty of the view that unfolded before my eyes. I turned to my wife and asked how anyone could fail to believe in God when witnessing his creation.

The psalmist made the same observation long ago: "The heavens proclaim His righteousness; all the peoples see His glory" (Ps. 97:6). Paul, too, held that the glory of God in creation renders every man accountable. "From the creation of the world His invisible attributes, that is, His eternal power and divine nature, have been clearly seen, being understood through what He has made. As a result, people are without excuse" (Rom. 1:20).

The beauty in creation is indeed utterly breathtaking. Everyone can see it for themselves.

That's why the Lord warned his people against the use of material things as images of deity, as idols to be worshipped. "Do not make an idol for yourself, whether in the shape of anything in the heavens above or on the earth below or in the waters under the earth. You must not bow down to them or worship them" (Exod. 20:4–5a). God wanted them to see that nature receives its glory from him. Nature's beauty, strength, and grandeur are expressions of its Creator, not ends in themselves to be worshipped and revered above the one, or *instead* of the one, who made them (Lev. 19:4, 21:6; Deut. 4:15–19; 5:8–10).

The New Testament, however, speaks of a more subtle form of idolatry—of hoarding and ascribing stand-alone value to material things.

Jesus warned against laying up treasure on earth, basing his statement on a fundamental truth: "No one can be a slave of two masters, since either he will hate one and love the other, or be devoted to one and despise the other. You cannot be slaves of God and of money" (Matt. 6:24).

You remember, too, the parable Jesus told about the big fool with the little barn (Luke 12:13–21), the man who had made earthly riches his ultimate goal. This businessman had made a significant miscalculation, however, in assuming that he would possess all his material wealth even after death. He had stored up earthly treasure, but his heart was not rich toward God.

The rich young ruler provided another example of Jesus' teaching on the proper use of money and possessions (Mark 10:17–31). He required the man to sell all and give to the poor precisely because Jesus knew that this person had made wealth his master.

So not only does creation reflect God's glory; it must be managed in such a manner that it serves his sovereign purpose, bringing "everything together in the Messiah, both things in heaven and things on earth in Him" (Eph. 1:10).

All created things, including man, have one ultimate purpose—the glory of God. We are called to live in such a manner that all the resources he has made available to us are used to glorify him. We all know that, even if we don't always like what it costs us.

But see if you like the thought of this: Although we cannot maintain our hold on material wealth after our death, we can even today be using the fleeting provisions of this world to make a kingdom impact that will last long after we're gone.

This is the added bonus and privilege of God's good creation.

For Our Good

There can be little doubt that man is the climax of God's creative activity. The world and all that is in it have been prepared for man's habitation, for his use and his joy. But again, this truth requires a balance in our thinking and perspective.

On the one hand, we see the incredible generosity of God, who through his grace has brought us into existence as living beings made in his own image, providing for our every need. Yet the moment we declare this, we must remember that our chief end is to serve God's purposes, not our own—to glorify him, not ourselves.

Leo Green lists four aspects of man's relationship to this material world.

1. *First, he notes that it is provided for man's existence.* The material world is essential to our survival, providing for the sustenance of the body and the stability of the mind and emotions. It is true that man cannot live by bread alone, but it is equally true that he cannot live without any bread at all! There is something altogether holy in Jesus' instruction to his disciples to pray for daily bread. It reminded them that their ability to focus on God's kingdom was totally reliant on his daily provision.[5]

2. *Second, the world is provided for man's enjoyment.* The word *Eden* means "delight, happiness, bliss." In the Old Testament the relationship between the Israelites and their material things was dominated by joy. God's intention is that we enjoy his good creation and thus live in gratitude and trust.

3. *Third, creation has been designed for man's enrichment.* Nature, when rightly perceived, can become a medium of revelation. You might want

to read Psalm 8, 19, or 104 at this point. If you are familiar with the Old Testament book of Job, you will recall that God used nature (chapters 38–41) to point Job to himself.

4. *Finally, the material world proves an instrument for self-expression.* Green writes, "Through 'created things' man can express his creative abilities in work (Genesis 1–2, etc.), and his devotion to God and his kingdom in worship."[6]

I would even add to this list two more things that naturally flow out of the first four.

5. *Material things provide the means and opportunity of man's development and maturation* as he learns to manage that which has been given to him in stewardship.

6. *Finally and above all, material things provide the opportunity and means by which man can participate in God's kingdom activity on planet Earth.*

And all of these things fall back in line with stewardship. Recognizing that we are part of the world of creation should create in us a reverence for all life. Recognizing that we are the stewards of all but the owners of nothing should save us from falling into the trap of secularism and consumerism.

When we become *preoccupied* with things rather than *mastering* things, we are doomed to become their slaves. Thus, we must learn restraint, balance, perspective, and stewardship.

And this is all very good.

Created in His Image

Then God said, "Let Us make man in Our image, according to Our likeness.
They will rule the fish of the sea, the birds of the sky, the animals, all the
earth, and the creatures that crawl on the earth."

GENESIS 1:26

Whenever you're feeling insignificant, undervalued, or depressed, just read this verse and absorb this singular truth: *God created everything with you in mind.* You are of inestimable value because you have been created in the image of God.

You can't read the first chapter of Genesis and not realize that verses 26–28 indicate that man was the zenith of creation. After God provided a total environment designed for man's good, he declared his intention to create man in his own image, both male and female. Nothing else can claim the birthright of being made in the image of God, of being singled out for special relationship with him and with his created order.

We are God's agent on the earth. We are the world's caretaker.

When you read Genesis 1, you notice that man shares the sixth day of creation with other living creatures, such as livestock, crawling things, and wildlife (1:24). They are made from the same "stuff" as man—the dust of the earth (2:7, 19), and they are told with a similar blessing to reproduce after their kind (1:22, 28).

But the main emphasis here is not on the similarities but on the differences. In verse 24 we find the phrase, "Let the earth produce living creatures according to their kinds," in reference to God's creation of the animal kingdom. But in verse 26 we read, not "Let the earth produce" but "Let Us make."

Mankind is in a class by himself.

This does not suggest that God was uninvolved in the creation of the animals. But it does indicate his loving and personal attention to the creation of man, who alone is made in his own image.

Bible teachers actually differ somewhat over the significance of the plural "our" in describing man being made "in Our image." Some see the plural as simply emphasizing the sovereign majesty of God. The early church fathers and the later reformers took this as a reference to an intra-Trinity dialogue. Other teachers argue that while we cannot derive a doctrine of the Trinity from this use of the plural, it does nonetheless suggest a plurality in the Godhead.

If so, the use of the plural "our" followed by the singular "his" would emphasize both the plurality *and* the unity of the Godhead.

The involvement in creation of the triune God is clearly taught in Scripture. In Genesis 1:2 we are told that the Spirit of God was hovering over the surface of the waters. Proverbs 8:30 speaks of "personified wisdom" (often identified with Christ) as being a coparticipant in creation. Paul makes clear that everything was created through Christ and for Christ (Col. 1:16b).

But no matter what line of interpretation you draw from this mystery, one thing we know: God, the three in one, created the world for you and then created you in his own image.

The two phrases "in Our image, according to Our likeness" (Gen. 1:26) are bold affirmations proclaiming that God has a plan and purpose for your life. And while these verses do not specifically describe the contents of the "image of God," there are clear indications in the context to aid us in knowing at least some of what that means.

And inside this understanding, we discover rich insights into our stewardship privilege.

What Is Man?

1. *Man is relational.* Genesis 2 tells the story of the beginning with a focus on the creation of man. Verse 18 of that chapter contains a telling phrase: "It is not good for the man to be alone. I will make a helper who is like him." This verse is then immediately followed by the task of naming the animals. "But for the man no helper was found who was like him" (2:20).

On the surface it is a bit humorous that God told man he was creating a helper for him and then paraded the animals past him one by one. This process made abundantly clear that among the animals no helper would be suitable for him. Man was the unique one, created for intimate and intentional relationship with one like himself, one who was also created in the image of God. Thus, when woman was created, the man said; "This one, at last, is bone of my bone, and flesh of my flesh" (2:23).

We are not designed to be "alone" creatures. We demand and desire the fellowship of others like ourselves. Thus the union of one man and one woman is the absolute standard (v. 24). We have been designed and destined to seek relationships with others created in the image of God.

But our greatest relational need is to live in intimacy with our Creator. In Genesis 3:8 we are given a glimpse of the relationship man was allowed to have with God: "The man and his wife heard the sound of the LORD God walking in the garden at the time of the evening breeze." God had created them with the capacity and desire to know and please their Creator. It was this profound truth that inspired the famous statement of Pascal, the French philosopher, who spoke of the God-shaped vacuum in the human heart.

We cannot live fully without God because we have been created by him and for him. Our life and purpose are found in him alone.

2. *Man is rational.* Simply stated, we have been created with the ability to understand and respond to God's revelation. Genesis 2:9 indicates that God provided for all of man's needs and placed two special trees in the midst of the garden—the tree of life and the tree of the knowledge of good and evil. Then the Lord commanded the man, "You are free to eat from any tree of the garden, but you must not eat from the tree of the knowledge of good and evil, for on the day you eat from it, you will certainly die" (2:16–17).

The garden was designed to foster the full development of man's spiritual, physical, and aesthetic appetites. But for his spiritual development, he was given a divine word that contained both commandment and prohibition, both permission and restriction. He was free to eat of every tree but one. The animals, of course, inhabited the garden with *no* such restrictions because they lack the capacity to comprehend and understand the command of their Creator in the same way man does. Man is unique. We can both hear and respond to God. We are rational beings.

3. *Man is responsible.* God's first words to the man and woman were words of blessing, followed by the assignment, "Be fruitful, multiply, fill the earth, and subdue it. Rule the fish of the sea, the birds of the sky, and every creature that crawls on the earth" (1:28).

The idea of *responsibility* is implied in both the blessing and the assignment, as is its partner, *accountability.* Man was given dominion over the created order, implying that he was responsible to his Creator to manage the world according to the design and desire of God.

This remains true. We have been appointed as God's royal representatives to rule the earth in his place. The words *subdue* and *rule* do not imply possession in terms of ownership. We find no suggestion anywhere in Scripture that God transferred his ownership of the earth to man. Our ownership must always be understood as *delegated* ownership.

Therefore, we own nothing, as well as everything—"nothing" in an absolute sense but "everything" in terms of our assigned stewardship. We have *secondary* dominion under the *absolute* dominion of our Lord, Creator, and King.

And here we see these three elements all at once—man's relational, rational, and responsible qualities—coming together to create our role as stewards. As relational beings, we find ourselves needing fellowship with God and with others. As rational beings, we have the capacity to understand God's revelation in which he gives us his standards for the use of all material things. Therefore, we have been given the responsibility to manage the King's resources in accordance with those standards and for his stated purposes.

We are his stewards.

We have already introduced the word *stewardship* without really defining it. Literally, a steward is a "house manager" (cp. Luke 16:2). The verb form of that word means "to divide, distribute, or apportion." The rich man in Jesus' parable (Luke 16:1–9) ordered his steward to "give an account of your management" (v. 2). In other words, he was calling for his books and records.

The most fundamental requirement for a steward is that he "be found faithful" (1 Cor. 4:2). So our responsibility for the created order implies ultimate accountability for it. Therefore, it stands to reason that we must understand *subdue* and *rule* in terms of *proper use,* never in terms of *abuse.* Christians are sometimes accused of not caring about the earth, of not being outspoken and active enough in ecological causes. The truth is, our biblical mandate requires us to be more concerned than *anyone* about our care for God's natural resources, as long as in the process we do not elevate creation into a god to be worshipped and served above the Creator.

Blessing and Mission

God's first words to humankind, "Let Us make man in Our image" so that "they will rule" (Gen. 1:26) over all creation as its stewards, are words that contain both *blessing* and *mission*.

When we think of blessing, we often focus on the gift but ignore our responsibility for how we handle or use it—the mission aspect of it. And while the biblical view of blessing certainly contains the idea of physical gifts bestowed upon man, the mission is ultimately the greatest gift of all. The fact that the sovereign God of the universe allows us to serve as his royal stewards over all creation is blessing enough.

When we study the story of Abraham, Isaac, Jacob, and Moses, we find that the promise of blessing always contains these twin elements—both provision and mission. In fact, in the story of the call of Abraham, we probably find this formula of blessing and mission more clearly stated than anywhere else: "I will make you into a great nation, I will bless you, I will make your name great, and you will be a blessing. . . . All the peoples on earth will be blessed through you" (Gen. 12:2, 3b).

Even as early as Genesis 2, as part of the description of the Garden of Eden, we are given a hint of a larger world that exists beyond its borders, a land fed by streaming rivers and filled with diversity of natural resources like gold and onyx. This is perhaps our earliest glimpse at the mission of reaching beyond ourselves to the other people of the world, of man's growing responsibility to advance the kingdom beyond comfortable boundaries.

The psalmist asked, "What is man that God would remember him and look after him?" Then he responded to his own question. "You made him little less than God and crowned him with glory and honor. You made him lord over the works of Your hands; You put everything under his feet" (Ps. 8:5–6).

God created man in his image to be the *recipient* of his blessing so that we can in turn be the *conduit* of his blessing.

The Impact of the Fall

The ground is cursed because of you. You will eat from it by means of painful labor all the days of your life.

GENESIS 3:17B

Sin changes everything. And don't we all know it from personal observation and experience.

That's why it's impossible for us even to imagine what the original garden must have been like. The thought of a place where every need was provided for, where man was given the privilege of walking with God in unrestrained, guiltless freedom—it seems too good to be true. Even today we speak of beautiful, idyllic situations as being like the garden of Eden.

But what we see around us today is not like that. Something drastic has happened to the created order that God himself declared to be "very good." Instead of an easy tending of natural resources to occupy our day, we find ourselves struggling to make a living, clinging tenaciously to that which is "ours," often fighting over money.

So before we can truly understand our stewardship of material possessions, we must first understand the impact of sin on our attitudes and environment. We must take into account the rebellion of man and the resulting fall.

The Temptation

Eve fell to the temptation of an inferior being whose malevolent brilliance suggested he was a tool of the devil, the great adversary of man. Notice the subtlety of the serpent's temptation. He began with a suggestion that caused Eve to question whether she had heard God right. "Did God really say, 'You can't eat from any tree in the garden'?" (3:1), the serpent asked. The implication was clear—a loving God wouldn't withhold anything good from man, would he?

Of course, the serpent intentionally misquoted God, suggesting that he didn't want man eating from *any* tree, focusing on God's one prohibition while ignoring his generosity in giving them everything necessary for life. Even today, temptation and rebellion begin the moment we doubt God's goodness and believe that his Word is subject to our judgment.

Eve was being drawn into that web in verse 2. She agreed with the tempter, even adding to and exaggerating God's restriction, telling the serpent that God had said, "You must not eat it *or touch it*" (v. 3).

The confrontation was now becoming even more direct and intentional, with the serpent contradicting the Word of God. "No! You will not die," the tempter declared (v. 4). Therefore, the woman was forced to choose—to believe the word of the serpent or to believe the Word of God.

This seems like such a no-brainer, we find it difficult to believe she would fall for an obvious lie rather than trusting the Word of the loving God, who had created her and provided for her every need. But when we reject God's principles about our use of Earth, do we not also repeat Eve's error?

The climax of the enemy's temptation is one we are all familiar with: "Your eyes will be opened and you will be like God, knowing good and evil" (v. 5). It is intoxicating to think that we can be godlike.

I can hear some of you saying, "Aw, come on. No one really believes he knows as much about life as the Creator does." Perhaps! But while we would never be so brazen as to make such an assertion in words, we do make a habit of pitting our knowledge against God when we ignore his Word and follow our own "wisdom."

And there is perhaps no single area where we are more tempted to do so than in the arena of our finances.

The Fall

Verse 6 states the Fall in such simple terms that we're astounded man found it so easy to rebel against his Creator. Eve saw that the fruit was delightful to look at, she desired it, and thus she took it. I have to admit that I struggle with the same progression toward sin. It begins with sight, which creates desire. Desire leads us somehow to conclude that we need it, deserve it, or just want it. So we take it.

Derek Kidner has summarized the issue succinctly: "The pattern of sin runs right through the act. For Eve listened to a creature instead of the Creator, followed her impressions against her instructions, and made self-fulfillment her goal. This prospect of material, aesthetic, and mental enrichment seemed to add up to life itself."[7]

Adam, too, rather than taking the lead in obedience and righteousness, followed his wife into sin. The man and woman bought the lie! They believed they could rely on their wisdom rather than obeying God's Word. Mankind's "yes" to God's singular "no" occurs when we reinterpret earthly greatness in terms of greed rather than trust.

The Consequences

The results of ignoring God's Word in the garden were immediate, extensive, and far-reaching. They reach even to us today. Man, as we saw in the last chapter, was created in the image of God and designed to be relational, rational, and responsible. Therefore, the Fall yielded consequences in all three of these areas. The joy of ruling over God's created order felt the full sting of sin.

The first and overarching loss was the relationship the man and woman enjoyed with their Creator. Can you imagine the joy they must have felt in the days before the Fall when they heard the sound of the Lord walking in the garden? That original sense of excitement was now replaced by fear and shame. They hid from their Creator since they were afraid because of their nakedness (vv. 8–9). Why would they think to hide their nakedness from God who created them and knew their inmost being? Rebellion always works itself out in terms of fear and shame.

The second loss was the relationship the man and woman shared with each other. Quickly, we begin to see enmity and blame develop between them. The very one whom Adam declared to be "bone of my bone, and flesh of my flesh" (2:23), he now blames for causing him to sin. The woman in turn blames the serpent. But implicit in both responses is the suggestion that this whole mess is God's fault. Hear it in Adam's statement: "The woman You gave to be with me" (v. 12a)—*it's her fault!*

The seeds of doubt sown by the serpent had borne full fruit, and the man and woman doubted that God had their best interest at heart. The intimacy of relationship with God and with each other was now clouded by the impact of sin.

It still is.

Our rebellion against God's standards—think of this in terms of stewardship—always issues from a sense of doubt that God truly understands our circumstances and knows what is best for us. Thus we continue to trust our devices rather than obey God's Word.

Adam and Eve certainly understood to some extent the enormity of our sin, but they wanted to put the blame elsewhere and avoid the consequences of their actions. Yet, because the flip side of rationality is responsibility, God informed them of the consequences of their sin. Pain and dissension would appear on the horizon for their marital relationship, as the woman would experience travail in childbirth. The phrase "Your desire will be for your husband, yet he will dominate you" (v. 16) indicates a relationship which would slip from the personal realm of "love and cherish" to one of instinctive passions such as "desire and dominate."

Man was intended to rule over the material world in joyful partnership with God. But after the Fall, man's task became wearisome toil (vv. 17–19). Concepts like "painful labor" (v. 17) and "sweat of your brow" (v. 19) began to make an appearance. And as you keep reading the stories of this first family, you will find that the impact of the Fall continued. Distrust. Selfishness. Jealousy. Murder. Misery.

Yes, that which was intended to be used in cooperation with the Creator was now hoarded and abused. Rather than turning to God, mankind concluded that the only way to survive was to make a name for himself by building a monument to his own ego (Gen. 11:4). Man's rebellion resulted in his proclivity to cry out "mine" rather than "thine."

The Continuing Saga

The impact of sin on man's relationship to his Creator and the creation continued unabated throughout the pages of Scripture and the history of man, affecting among other things our stewardship of what God has given us. We now see conclusions like these as the normal human response to money and wealth.

1. *That which was created "good" is frequently the occasion for sin.* Man's selfishness causes a savage rape of the earth and its natural resources. The land, seas, and the atmosphere are polluted as man reinterprets "dominion" in terms of selfish abuse rather than responsible stewardship. Paul would

later declare: "For we know that the whole creation has been groaning together with labor pains until now" (Rom. 8:22).

2. *Man begins to accumulate rather than manage and distribute.* The nature of God is to give, and he designed the world to be "giving." The sun gives light, the earth gives food, and the animals produce after their kind. But fallen man chooses to consume rather than convey. The prophets frequently condemned those who oppressed the poor to gain wealth. "Woe to those who add house to house and join field to field until there is no more room and you alone are left in the land" (Isa. 5:8).

One of the most telling stories of the Old Testament is the account of King Ahab's irrational desire for the vineyard of Naboth (1 Kings 21). A wealthy king who owned everything a man could desire was unhappy because Naboth refused to sell him the one thing he really wanted, his small vineyard. And because Ahab's appetite for stuff had become insatiable (as ours can become) and because what he would do to obtain it had become despicable, Ahab had Naboth killed in order to possess it!

The New Testament tells the story of the big fool with the little barn who thinks only of accumulation and fails to understand that he is really only a manager (Luke 12:18). All of his calculations came to nothing when he was held responsible by the true owner.

3 *Man's greed leads to exploitation rather than cooperation.* I encourage you to put down this book for a moment and read all of Leviticus 25. All of God's directives concerning the land in that chapter have at their heart God's concern for his people. "The land will yield its fruit, so that you can eat, be satisfied, and live securely in the land" (v. 19). Another point is clearly articulated in this section: the land belongs to the Lord. As managers—not owners—Israel was intended to work in cooperation with God, the true owner, to manage it by his directives for their own good. Later Jeremiah would declare that God would punish Israel with the loss of the land because they had exploited it rather than managed it (Jer. 25).

4. *Man's affection for his Creator is supplanted by his desire for the physical creation.* The desire for wealth is so seductive that it can keep us from God. The listening crowd was startled when Jesus declared, "How hard it is for those who have wealth to enter the kingdom of God" (Mark 10:23). Do you remember the context? We had just been introduced to the rich young ruler, who would be the poster boy of success for our day. When the young man asked what he must do to inherit eternal life, Jesus told him to sell all he had and to give it to the poor. It is certainly fair to suggest that this passage demonstrated Jesus' concern for the poor, but it means more than that. Jesus did not require that all those who wanted to follow him must dispose of all

their wealth. The text makes clear that Jesus' requirement was prompted by his love for this one young man as an individual (v. 21). Jesus could see this man's slavery to wealth, the tyranny of riches. Thus he demanded of him, as he does of all would-be disciples in every generation, to surrender anything and everything that would claim his first affection. As Paul would later say: "The love of money is a root of all kinds of evil" (1 Tim. 6:10a).

5. *Money is now a source of anxiety rather than blessing.* In the same section where Jesus taught the disciples how to pray, he warned them against laying up treasure on earth. The bottom line is that such treasure creates undue anxiety. Someone can break in and steal it, or moths and rust can corrupt it. But the bigger issue at stake is this: "For where your treasure is, there your heart will be also" (Matt. 6:21).

He then illustrated his point from nature by pointing at the birds and the lilies, contrasting the difference between a life that is effortless and a life that is strained. Anxiety comes when we attempt to force life events into a pattern of our own making. When we allow wealth to become our god, we are rewarded by anxiety and uneasiness. We are doomed to spend our time taking care of our god, protecting it from moth, rust, and thieves. The choice is pretty clear: we can either choose to serve God who can take care of you, or we can spend our days anxiously taking care of the god of our own making.

Bishop Sheen said that those who make material things their god exhibit three characteristics. They have a passionate desire to accumulate, they are reluctant to give, and they feel the world owes them a living.[8] That's why Jesus counseled, "But seek first the kingdom of God and His righteousness, and all these things will be provided for you" (Matt. 6:33).

6. *The world is now in rebellion against the Creator.* The great irony of the Fall is that the term *world* has come to describe the creation in rebellion against God. As John wrote, "Do not love the world or the things that belong to the world. If anyone loves the world, the love for the Father is not in him. Because everything that belongs to the world—the lust of the flesh, the lust of the eyes, and the pride in one's lifestyle—is not from the Father, but is from the world" (1 John 2:15–16). How far different and twisted this is from God's original design for creation.

What a legacy! Enmity between God and man, multiplied sorrow for women, the ground cursed, man banished from the garden, man's opportunity for kingdom stewardship cast into chaos!

But don't despair, for there is yet another chapter to be written.

The Creator is also the Redeemer.

Week 1, Day 5

Redemption and the Material World

I will put hostility between you and the woman, and between your seed and her seed. He will strike your head, and you will strike his heel.

GENESIS 3:15

The Bible begins with the story of the first creation, "In the beginning God created the heavens and the earth" (Gen. 1:1), and ends with the story of the new creation, "Then I saw a new heaven and a new earth, for the first heaven and the first earth had passed away, and the sea existed no longer" (Rev. 21:1).

Everything in between is about God's relentless love and his plan to bring redemption to the earth.

The word *redemption* is a beautiful word, but it implies a price be paid. Some of you may be old enough to remember the redemption centers where we used to trade Green Stamp books for some product. Others of you may identify more closely with a pawn shop, where a person can go to "buy back" an object he once owned. God owns us by virtue of creation, but because of our sin and the resulting fall, we became owned by another.

He paid the highest price to buy us back.

The Genesis Promise

Because of his rebellion, man was driven from the Garden of Eden, and reentry wasn't simply made more difficult but was made impossible. "He drove man out, and east of the garden of Eden He stationed cherubim with a flaming, whirling sword to guard the way to the tree of life" (Gen. 3:24). While the punishment must have seemed harsh to the first couple, God's grace was already at work. Sinful man could not approach a holy God in his sinful condition, and so God in his mercy prohibited man from approaching him until the price of redemption was paid.

But we must not skip over the promise contained in Genesis 3:15. This verse is often called the *protoevangelium* or "first glimpse of the gospel." Paul later unveiled the identity of the serpent in Romans 16:20, when he wrote, "The God of peace will soon crush Satan under your feet." Yes, it was Satan who had bruised the heel of the woman's seed, but in the process his head was to be crushed under the weight of another.

It is not incidental that the serpent bypassed man and attacked the seed of the woman, for through the seed of the woman ultimate redemption was to come. Paul wrote, "But when the completion of the time came, God sent His Son, born of a woman, born under the law, to redeem those under the law, so that we might receive the adoption as sons" (Gal. 4:4; cp. Matt. 1:23).

The serpent was instrumental in the Fall of the woman, and the enmity between the serpent and her seed have continued throughout history. The language of the passage suggests intense hostility, a life-and-death struggle. It is not surprising that the serpent struck at the heel since he was relegated to move on his belly all the days of his life. But the impact of striking at the heel of the seed of the woman caused the final destruction of the serpent. While one is cautious to read too much into an Old Testament reference, it is difficult not to see the cross in this story. When Satan thought he had dealt the decisive blow to the seed of the woman, his act brought ultimate redemption and thus his own destruction.

Redemption Restores Relationship

Man was created to live in intimate relationship with his Creator, but his sin resulted in banishment from the garden and a broken relationship with his Creator. This marred the image of God that had been created in man.

But it didn't render it totally lost.

In Genesis 9:6, when God was establishing a new post-flood covenant with Noah and his family—an event that certainly occurred after the Fall—God warned against the shedding of man's blood, "for God made man in His image." Much later James would also warn against an inappropriate use of the tongue to curse other people, based on the truth that man is created in God's image (James 3:9).

The redemption of mankind was a costly transaction. Sin not only created a barrier between sinful man and holy God but also created a debt which had to be paid. Paul indicated that the "wages of sin is death" (Rom. 6:23). Thankfully, that statement is immediately followed by the wonderful promise, "But the gift of God is eternal life in Christ Jesus our Lord." But the promise of eternal life means that someone had to pay the debt of sin. And as Paul tells us, God the Father "made the One who did not know sin to be sin for us, so that we might become the righteousness of God in Him" (2 Cor. 5:21).

So here's the whole story—a review for those of you who have experienced it, and a reminder of the great news we can carry into our world to share with others. "When you were dead in trespasses and in the uncircumcision of your flesh, He made you alive with Him and forgave us all our trespasses. He erased the certificate of debt . . . against us and opposed to us, and has taken it out of the way by nailing it to the cross. He disarmed the rulers and authorities and disgraced them publicly; He triumphed over them by Him" (Col. 2:13–15).

He crushed the head of Satan at the cost of his Son.

Therefore, redemption has replaced estrangement with sonship. In Romans 8:15–17 Paul spoke of the spirit of slavery and fear being replaced by adoption, allowing us to cry out, "Abba, Father." The Spirit now bears testimony to our spirit that we are children and heirs. Even though our faith requires that we suffer with him, we know we will also be glorified with him.

Interestingly, the Bible speaks of man's redemption in terms of "a new creation" (2 Cor. 5:17; Gal. 6:15) and new birth (John 3:8). So it is not surprising that sonship and glory are closely related to each other in the New Testament. The glory of the Lord speaks of his manifest presence. In other words, new birth brings about the restoration of the image of God in man. "We all, with unveiled faces, are reflecting the glory of the Lord and are being transformed into the same image from glory to glory; this is from the Lord who is the Spirit" (2 Cor. 3:18).

In Ephesians 4 Paul employed the imagery of putting to death the old man—our natural, sinful selves limited by the flesh and corrupted by deceitful desires. He then spoke of our process of renewal in these terms: "You put on the new man, the one created according to God's likeness, in righteousness and purity of the truth" (Eph. 4:24).

Paul also looked forward to the day when we who once bore the image of the "man made of dust" will bear "the image of the heavenly man" (1 Cor. 15:49). This radical transformation awaits the ultimate and full redemption of our bodies; but it begins the moment we put on that new man in Christ Jesus, the moment we become his new creation.

I can't afford to leave this section without asking you if you are certain you have been recreated in Christ. Have you been born again? It is a critical question, because flesh and blood cannot inherit the kingdom of God (1 Cor. 15:50). If you are not certain, please turn to the Appendix for a simple explanation of what this means and how you can receive it.

Redemption Alters Every Relationship

When sin invaded the garden, it impacted the human relationships of the first family and ultimately the relationship between man and his fellow-man. Thus we should not be startled to discover that redemption radically alters all our earthly relationships.

We can see this most clearly by a quick overview of several chapters of Paul's letter to the Ephesians. We have already looked at Ephesians 4:24, where Paul declared that we have put on the new man, but the instructions following this truth should be carefully noted, as well. Paul talked about speaking truth to our neighbors (v. 25), dealing with our anger (v. 26), working with our hands so that we might have resources to share with those in need (v. 28), and putting away filthy talk, bitterness, anger, wrath, insult, and slander (vv. 29–31). All of these things, including our kindness toward others, is anchored in and motivated by a fundamental truth: we are to respond to others with compassion and forgiveness because God forgave us in Christ (v. 32).

He then proceeded to talk about the relationships between husbands and wives, which should be marked by submission, respect, and love. He compared this relationship to the redemptive relationship Christ has with his church (Eph. 5:22–33). Further he talked about children and their parents. Children are to honor their parents in the Lord, and parents are to nurture their children with the training and instruction of God's way (Eph. 6:1–4). He goes further to talk about relationships at work (vv. 5–9), where man is told that he must reflect his obedience to Christ in the marketplace.

Yes, redemption is comprehensive in regard to one's relationships.

Redemption Brings New Focus

If nature suffered the consequences of sin, it stands to reason that it will enjoy the impact of redemption. We visited the prophet Ezekiel in an earlier study together—*Empowering Kingdom Growth: The Heartbeat of God*. This Old Testament prophet saw a coming day when God would give man a new heart and would put his own Spirit within him. Read the entire passage—Ezekiel 36—and you will see that the redemption of man was even to have an impact on man's relationship with the land. He talked about God's redeemed people living "in the land" (v. 28) and how God would "summon the grain and make it plentiful" (v. 29) so that his people would "no longer experience reproach among the nations on account of famine" (v. 30).

The images of fruitful living are abundant in Ezekiel 36. He told of cities being inhabited and the ruins rebuilt (v. 33), of desolate land being cultivated. In fact, the prophet indicated that everyone who passed by would compare the cultivated land to the "garden of Eden" (v. 35).

When this redemption of the land occurs and man has the created world back in its proper perspective, there will a profound result. "Then the nations that remain around you will know that I, the LORD, have rebuilt what was destroyed and have replanted what was desolate. I the LORD have spoken and I will do it" (v. 36). While redemption addresses all the issues of man's greatest needs, it is ultimately about the character and rule of God, of what he is accomplishing for his own name's sake.

Amos reflected this same hope of restoration for the land, picturing a bountiful harvest where the "plowman will overtake the reaper" and "the mountains will drip with sweet wine," where God's people will rebuild and he will "plant them on their land" (Amos 9:13–15). So if rebellion led to the loss of the land and man's stewardship of it, then redemption will surely allow man to live in a restored, fruitful relationship with the created world.

We have already mentioned the passage in Romans 8 where Paul talked about the creation groaning under the impact of sin until now. Listen to this text again: "For the creation eagerly waits with anticipation for God's sons to be revealed. . . . Creation itself will also be set free from the bondage of corruption into the glorious freedom of God's children" (8:19, 21).

It is fair to argue that the ultimate fulfillment of these promises awaits the return of the King, but it would be wrong to suggest that this process of renewal is not now at work in those who have already declared their allegiance to him, those in whose lives the kingdom is already at work.

In his first letter to the Corinthians, Paul declared that man doesn't have sufficient context to comprehend all that God has prepared for those who love him (2:9). Yet he notes that God has provided revelation to believers through his Spirit, who knows the deep things of God. He wrote, "We have not received the spirit of the world, but the Spirit who is from God, in order that we might know what has been freely given to us by God" (2:12). In other words, redeemed man is able once again to see the grace of all of life. The "graced man" acknowledges that all of life has been given to us in stewardship.

This profound understanding of the totality of redemption led Paul to exhort the Roman believers to present their bodies as a "living sacrifice." This is both pleasing to God and the reasonable response of one who has been redeemed. Such sacrifice enables us to overcome the pull of the world and allows us to be transformed by the renewing of our mind (Rom. 12:1–2). While the image has been restored, the pull of sin and the pressure of the world make daily renewal and transformation a necessity.

Jesus gave us a profound example of kingdom conversion with the story of Zacchaeus. This man was a rich tax collector (Luke 19:2), but the story implies that his wealth had not satisfied his basic need. To the chagrin of the crowd, Jesus invited himself to dinner with the tax collector. At some point in the evening Zacchaeus stood and declared: "Look, I'll give half of my possession to the poor, Lord! And if I have extorted anything from anyone, I'll pay back four times as much!" (v. 8). How did Jesus respond? "Today salvation has come to this house" (v. 9a). This passage does not suggest that Zacchaeus earned salvation by his good works. That would be contrary to the clear witness of Scripture. It does, however, indicate that true conversion will result in a restoration of man's understanding of his appropriate relationship to material possessions.

Kingdom Potential

Most if not all of what we've discussed in this chapter is familiar territory to you. But I share it again to help us see that our creation, our redemption, and our stewardship are inextricably bound together. Salvation is not just a matter of saving man's soul; it is about man as a whole. When we acknowledge the kingship of the Lord in redemption, it will of necessity affect all of life—our relationships and our stewardship of time, talents, gifts, opportunities, and money.

The material possessions God has given us have kingdom potential.

Redemption allows us to cry "Abba, Father," which indicates a filial level of trust. We are able to replace anxiety with trust because our passion for expanding our own kingdom has been replaced by our desire to seek his righteousness and his kingdom. In the process we discover that we can trust our Creator/Redeemer to provide for our needs.

But we can't conclude this week's study without facing a penetrating question Jesus asked Nicodemus. After telling him that one must be born again to enter the kingdom of God, Jesus assured Nicodemus that he spoke of things he knew by firsthand knowledge (John 3:11–13). He then asked: "If I have told you about things that happen on earth and you don't believe, how will you believe if I tell you about things of heaven?" (v. 12).

A laywoman in First Baptist Church, Norfolk, shared that this verse changed her understanding of stewardship. She explained that reading this verse had convicted her that if she was going to trust God with her eternal salvation, she must also be prepared to trust his Word as it related to her earthly behavior.

It is a haunting question, isn't it? Why do we so readily trust his Word when it comes to heavenly truth, and yet we struggle to obey it when it impacts our daily living?

This will be the question we'll face up close and personal the rest of the way.

The Purpose of Money

Week 2, Day 1

God's Heartbeat

You may say to yourself, "My power and my own ability
have gained this wealth for me," but remember that the LORD
your God gives you the power to gain wealth, in order to confirm
His covenant He swore to your fathers, as it is today.

DEUTERONOMY 8:17–18

Pride is an insidious enemy. It can cause us to forget the past and even take credit for that which was clearly not a matter of our own doing. Pride is heinous because it ignores the sheer grace of life, the reality that everything we are, everything we have, and everything we're able to do is a gift from God.

We may attempt to ignore or deny the fact that we are created by the King for his purpose and delight, but that does not alter the fundamental truth. We are! And if we belong to the King by virtue of both creation and redemption, then we have the power to use his created order to impact not only the world today but all eternity. Blessing is not simply a gift; it entails a mission.

And we see this truth unfold in God's first dealings with his people.

When God began to interact with Abraham and his descendants, he promised them a blessing that would make them a great nation. But this blessing given to Abraham entailed an accompanying responsibility or mission: "and all the peoples on earth will be blessed through you" (Gen. 12:3b). It is no exaggeration, then, to say that God's heartbeat is that all the nations of the earth come to know him as their rightful King. Thus it is critical that we understand how the blessing of God and the contingent resources that have been placed into our stewardship are to be employed for this kingdom task.

First Steps

As we read through the book of Genesis, we find that much of the patriarchal period was marked by consumption of blessing with little regard to the mission to the nations. We end the book of Genesis with Israel experiencing a great famine over all the land. They are forced to go to Egypt for provision, and in due time they find themselves in bondage to a pharaoh who does not know Joseph (Exod. 1:8).

The book of Exodus opens with the story of the oppression of Israel in Egyptian bondage. Even in captivity God continues to bless them, and the Israelites grow in number in spite of the hard labor and the plans of the pharaoh to destroy the male children. Then God calls Moses to be their deliverer, to redeem their nation; and God fortifies him with the promise of his presence and the revelation of his memorial name (Exod. 3:14).

After a lengthy showdown with the pharaoh and his supposed gods, the Israelites are allowed to leave Egypt. But the pharaoh then changes his mind and rallies his army to stop the Israelites. God miraculously delivers Israel by opening the Red Sea, allowing his people to cross on dry land.

Certainly you already know this story. But stay with me as we see it through new eyes, through the lens of stewardship and our own responsibility to use God's resources in ways that reflect his purposes, that track with his heartbeat.

In the commissioning of Moses, God had assured him that he would allow Israel to worship him at a particular mountain (Exod. 3:12). For three months they traveled, experiencing daily God's miraculous provision for their every need. As they worshipped God, he established a covenant with them, making them his own possession, a kingdom of priests, and a holy nation (Exod. 19:5–6), to be the earthly representative of the rightful King over all the earth. And God promised that he would provide the resources for them to fulfill their mission.

Much of the imagery of God's provision is related to the promise of an abundantly fruitful land. The phrase "milk and honey" occurs twenty times to describe the lavish material provisions he had made for his covenant people in the Promised Land. Hear it in its first iteration: "I have come down to rescue them from the power of the Egyptians and to bring them from that land to a good and spacious land, a land flowing with milk and honey" (Exod. 3:8a).

In the book of Numbers, we find God's people on the banks of the Jordan, poised and ready to take the land provided for them by God. Moses sent scouts into the land to check it out. Their conclusion—"We went into the land where you sent us. Indeed it is flowing with milk and honey, and here is some of its fruit" (Num. 13:27). Tragically this positive report is followed by a "however" or a "but." Some of the scouts complain that the inhabitants of the land are large and the cities are fortified. The bottom line, Israel refuses to possess the land that God has already provided for them.

Therefore, they must submit to God's judgment, wandering in the wilderness until an entire unbelieving and unresponsive generation had died. Finally, in the book of Deuteronomy, we find Israel once again poised to enter the land. Moses is preparing to give the reins of leadership to Joshua, but first he must provide a new generation with a history lesson and a challenge.

Pause a moment to reflect. Have you ever responded to one of God's promises with a *however* or a *but*? What was the result?

The Dangerous Risk

Deuteronomy 8 opens with a stern reminder: "You must carefully follow every command I am giving you today, so that you may live and increase, and may enter and take possession of the land the LORD swore to your fathers" (v. 1). Two themes are found throughout this section— obedience and praise—the pathway and response to blessing.

In verse 6 he reminds them, "Keep the commands of the LORD your God by walking in His ways and fearing Him." The reminder to obey is immediately followed by a description of the land, which goes far beyond the mere mention of "milk and honey." It is a land with wheat, barley, vines, figs, pomegranates, olive oil, and more—"a land where you will eat food without shortage, where you will lack nothing" (v. 9). Their appropriate response to such largesse? "When you eat and are full, you will praise the LORD your God for the good land He has given you" (v. 10).

Obedience. Praise. These are our obligations for such lavish generosity.

But the Lord knows our hearts, our inclinations, and our natural, forget- ful reactions. Following the description of God's abundant provision, Moses grabbed their attention by repeating the statement, "Be careful" (vv. 11, 14). In the first instance he told them to be careful not to forget the Lord by failing to obey his Word, not because hardship would drive them to it but rather abundance. Then as now we are just as likely (or perhaps even more likely) to ignore God in times of plenty as we are in times of shortage.

So Moses warned them, "When you eat and are full, and build beautiful houses to live in, and your herds and flocks grow large, and your silver and gold multiply, and everything else you have increases, *be careful* that your heart doesn't become proud and you forget the LORD your God who brought you out of the land of Egypt, out of the place of slavery" (vv. 12–14).

When we are not careful to obey God's Word about the use of his resources, we are liable to become proud in our hearts, forgetting that all of life is grace.

Moses was aware that the blessings and abundance of the land might lull the people into a sense of self-sufficiency, pride, and complacency. They may actually begin to think, "My power and my own ability have gained this wealth for me" (v. 17).

I know that none of us are ever tempted to think that we gain our wealth by our own strength, or are we? Do you ever pat yourself on the back for your hard work and industry? Do you sometimes applaud yourself for an astute investment? Ever find yourself tempted to think that what I have is "mine"?

Such attitudes can cause us to worship wealth—when we think of it as ours, when we hoard it as if it provides our security, when we consume it rather than convey it, when we use it for our pleasure and ignore God's mission.

There is dire warning for those who forget that God is the one who gives the power to gain wealth. "If you ever forget the LORD your God and go after other gods to worship and bow down to them, I testify against you today that you will perish" (v. 19).

Blessing or Cursing—Our Choice

We enjoy singing and talking about God's *blessing*, but the thought of God's *cursing* is alien to our ears. Yet before this new generation of Israelites were allowed to take the land, God laid before them a choice and a consequence. "Look, today I set before you a blessing and a curse; there will be a blessing, if you obey the commands of the LORD your God I am giving you today, and a curse, if you do not obey the commands of the LORD your God" (Deut. 11:26–28a).

If the blessing of God involves his presence, his provision, and his protection, then his cursing means man's forfeiture of the same. It is not so much that God withholds blessing as it is that we reject it.

Let me make sure I'm being clear about what's involved in this "cursing" of God. It's not so much the active removal of his presence, provision, and protection from our lives as it is our *moving ourselves out from under them.* Much of this curse is something we bring on ourselves.

It's like a parent who fences in the backyard to protect his young children when they're riding their tricycles. If they obediently remain in the secure area, they will be safe. But if they remove themselves from the boundaries of protection, they open themselves to risk and harm.

Wasn't this the consequences of Adam and Eve's rebellion? This wasn't simply a punishment decreed by an outside source. They forfeited the joy of God's presence, the garden of his provision, and the power of his protection. God's law, like his garden, is designed for man's good. Thus, when we ignore or disobey his Word, we are sure to experience the consequences.

This is evidence of our covenant with him.

The connection between covenant and blessing is clearly affirmed in Deuteronomy 8:18: "But remember that the LORD your God gives you the power to gain wealth, in order to confirm His covenant He swore to your fathers." Israel was reminded that every blessing in life they enjoyed was the direct result of the promise God had made to their forefathers.

This verse does not suggest that prosperity is essential to covenant reality. That would fly in the face of covenant theology. God's covenant love flows from his amazing grace and is undeserved by all.

Neither does it suggest that those *lacking* wealth are excluded from the blessings of God. Such an understanding would not only cut out a great proportion of the world's population but would make nonsensical God's concern for the poor.

Further, it does not teach that prosperity is a sign of God's pleasure and that a lack thereof indicates his displeasure. We must be careful not to fall into the trap of the health, wealth, and success pundits.

What, then, does it mean?

First, it means that covenant people recognize and acknowledge that *all the resources we have come from the hand of God.* Second, it means that we have covenanted with him to use them *in accordance with his design and with his purpose in our hearts.*

Thus we must spend adequate time inquiring about what his design and purposes are. That, in fact, is our next assignment.

Meeting Needs, Providing Pleasure

*And my God will supply all your needs according the
His riches in glory in Christ Jesus.*

PHILIPPIANS 4:19

*Instruct those who are rich in the present age not to be arrogant
or to set their hope on the uncertainty of wealth, but on God
who richly provides us with all things to enjoy.*

1 TIMOTHY 6:17

How much is enough?

I had just arrived in Cambridge for my Ph.D. work. I knew nothing about the town but wanted to worship on my first Sunday morning in England. I had no mode of transportation other than my feet. So I started off through the park on my quest for a house of worship.

As you might expect, I quickly found a small Anglican church. The worship style was a bit awkward for a lifelong Southern Baptist, but the message was both biblical and convicting. The pastor quoted from a little book entitled *Enough Is Enough* and then proceeded to ask us how we determined how much was enough.

That question raised a couple of important issues that I have continued to ponder: What is the purpose of material possessions? And how do I handle that which God provides that goes beyond my basic needs?

We have already discovered that God designed the Garden of Eden as an environment in which all of man's needs were provided for. Further, we have discovered that God's blessing is often described in terms of abundance. The psalmist declared: "May there be plenty of grain in the land; may it wave on the tops of the mountains. May its crops be like Lebanon. May people flourish in the cities like the grass of the field" (Ps. 72:16).

The oft-repeated phrase "milk and honey" graphically portrays abundance. "Listen, Israel, and be careful to follow them [God's laws], so that you may prosper and multiply greatly, because the LORD, the God of your fathers, has promised you a land flowing with milk and honey" (Deut. 6:3).

Therefore, the possibility of abundance demands that the kingdom-focused person ask himself or herself, "How do I use that which goes beyond my basic needs?"

How much is enough?

The Meeting of Our Needs

First, let's underline the truth that a Christian may (in fact, must) use his God-provided resources to meet the necessities of life for himself and those dependent on him. The Lord acknowledged this need of ours for the necessities of life in the prayer we call the Lord's Prayer. The larger context indicates that "daily bread" means more than food. You remember Jesus' speaking a bit later in that passage from the Sermon on the Mount, not only about food but also clothing (Matt. 6:25, 28), the needs of our physical bodies (v. 26), and concerns about the future (v. 34). It is abundantly clear that God has provided us with material resources to meet our daily needs.

It is altogether appropriate to expect that from him.

Further, the context contrasts man's anxiety with the unconcern exhibited by nature, the birds of the sky and the flowers of the field. Jesus was not suggesting that we adopt the philosophy of life made popular by the memorable song from the Disney movie *The Lion King,* whose characters sing "Hakuna Matata," which means "no worries." Jesus did, however, give us an alternative to the strain and anxiety of living as if everything depends on our own industry and ingenuity. Because of God's love and provision, we can live with grateful confidence in the truth that everything we need will come to us from the hand of God.

The account of the prayer of Jesus in Luke 11—its other Gospel location—is followed by the story of a man with an unexpected, late-night guest and no provisions in his own house. So he awakens his neighbor, asking that he loan him three loaves of bread so that he can adequately provide for his company. The man's persistence is rewarded. Listen to the promise of provision: "He will get up and give him as much as he needs" (Luke 11:8).

And that's what God desires and has promised to provide—"as much as we need." Paul confirmed this caring quality of God's character by declaring that God will meet all our needs "according to His riches" (Phil. 4:19). Beyond comprehension, isn't it!

We should not ignore, however, that the prayer of Jesus contains three life commitments that precede the request for daily bread. These kingdom-focused mind-sets should become our driving force, our main priorities in life, freeing us from worry and ingratitude and the forgetfulness of natural man. They are:
- to embody his name,
- advance his kingdom,
- and accomplish his will.

Therefore, it doesn't take away from God's love for us as individuals to say that his provision for our daily needs is designed to sustain life and provide strength for kingdom activity. That's why Jesus ends this section of his teaching with a command laden with promise: "But seek first the kingdom of God and His righteousness and all these things will be provided for you" (Matt. 6:33).[1]

The Joy of Participation

Therefore, we, as responsible agents of God's creation, are given meaningful work for this purpose so that we may participate with him in providing for our own needs and those of the members of our own extended family.

Paul encountered a number of believers in Thessalonica whose anxious desire for the return of the Lord had caused them to give up their work. Paul's instruction to them was rather pointed and clear: "If anyone isn't willing to work, he should not eat" (2 Thess. 3:10). In other words, the promise of provision does not provide us with an excuse for laziness that sometimes masquerades as faith.

In another context Paul wrote to young Timothy, exhorting him to command those under his charge, "If anyone does not provide for his own relatives, and especially for his household, he has denied the faith and is worse than an unbeliever" (1 Tim. 5:8). The demand to care for one's extended family was made even more essential in ancient times by the absence of any retirement programs or welfare agencies. Thus, the godly man was enabled by God to work so that the material gain he received could be used to meet the basic necessities of life.

Providing for one's own family is an indisputable Christian duty. To forsake this would be a tacit denial of the faith, rendering one worse than an infidel. Even the pagan of the first century would have acknowledged his obligation to care for his own family. It would thus be unthinkable to live below pagan standards, particularly when one understands that he has been graciously allowed to manage God's resources in such a manner that enables him to provide for his family.

So anyone who thinks stewardship overrides this responsibility or demeans it as a waste or a drain on our giving has failed to heed the heartbeat of God. Providing for ourselves and our families is a clear command of Scripture. But it is not ours to do alone. The strength, initiative, knowledge, and health we need to carry out our daily tasks are in themselves gifts of God. It is his desire to meet our needs and for us to participate in the process.

Good to Enjoy

If you think about it, the meeting of our needs should really be sufficient to merit our highest praise. Not that working and sweating are always our favorite things to do, but the idea that we can and that God uses this as a means of quenching our most basic thirsts and hungers is praiseworthy indeed.

But it is also God's desire that we enjoy life.

We shouldn't forget that both the provision of the garden and man's responsibility for its management were deemed to be "very good." This indicates that God wants us to enjoy the work and the resulting provision that come from his hand. Paul's instruction to those who enjoy earthly wealth was to set their hope on God because he "provides us with all things to enjoy" (1 Tim. 6:17).

Jeremiah the prophet echoed this sentiment: "You will plant vineyards again on the mountains of Samaria; the planters will plant and will enjoy the fruit" (31:5). The book of Job stands as a stark reminder that we should not necessarily equate suffering with sin or prosperity with holiness. If you have read the book of Job, you know that his friends did not always give wise counsel. However, in the midst of one of Elihu's speeches, we find a nugget of gold. "If they serve Him obediently, they will end their days in prosperity and their years in happiness" (Job 36:11).

Paul frequently encountered those who thought deprivation was the way to fight fleshly indulgence and who approached life with a "thou shall not" mentality. In Colossians 2:21–23, he pointedly denounced the negatives of legalism. He declared that while those who promote an ascetic lifestyle have a reputation for wisdom, the negative practices they recommend are of no value against fleshly indulgence.

In 1 Timothy 4, Paul again spoke of those who forbid marriage and demand abstinence from food. Paul's antidote was this: everything created by God is to be received with thanksgiving (v. 4). In other words, to enjoy life we must first acknowledge that God is the Creator and giver; we are the recipient. Therefore, "the stuff of life" can be received as good and pleasurable "since it is sanctified by the word of God and by prayer" (v. 5).

This is God's heart.

Some think that Paul's use of the term "word of God" refers to Genesis 1:31, where God pronounced all his creation to be good. Others think that his connection of "word" and "prayer" in this verse points to the use of Scripture in the grace we say before meals. Such a practice certainly reminds us that God gives us all things to enjoy.

But I wonder if there might be an even more significant point here? If Jesus taught that prayer's earthly goal should be to advance God's kingdom—"Your kingdom come"—could the sanctification or "setting apart" of all things by prayer mean that we should understand, use, and enjoy all God's resources with the ultimate view that our purpose in life is to advance his kingdom?

Finding Contentment

The key issue in life is balance. When we talk about material possessions and enjoyment of life, we are really speaking about contentment.

Solomon gave us an insightful look into the issue of pleasure or enjoyment of life." In Ecclesiastes 2:1, he wrote that he set himself on a quest to discover pleasure. In short, this wealthy king had the resources to satiate all his senses. More than perhaps anyone else in human history, he had the unbridled means to seek the meaning of life in pleasure itself. His conclusion? "I said to myself, 'Go ahead, I will test you with pleasure and enjoy what is good.' But it turned out to be futile."

Later Solomon gave us a more mature reflection on life and the resources provided by God. He concluded that there is nothing better for man than enjoying the necessities of life and his labor—"for this will accompany him in his labor during the years of his days that God gives him under the sun" (8:15).

When one lives for pleasure, it becomes his elusive god. But when one lives for God, pleasure is discovered in the everyday relationships of life.

Paul echoed this same assessment. In 1 Timothy 5, he gave strong warning about the risk of desiring to be rich. Here's the real surprise, though—there are some who imagine that godliness is a way to material gain (5:5). But this only demonstrates how subtle the desire for wealth can be. Can you imagine someone practicing "godliness" for what they get out of it? Ouch! It is subtle! We can be tempted to teach or practice principles of stewardship with motives that are less than pure.

James even noted that sometimes we pray and don't receive what we ask for because our desire to receive is based on the hope and expectation that we can spend it on our own desires for pleasure (4:3). Are your prayers kingdom focused or earth centered? Are you always praying about your needs, or are you asking God to show you kingdom opportunities?

Paul gives a scriptural antidote: "But godliness with contentment is a great gain. For we brought nothing into the world, and we can take nothing out. But if we have food and clothing, we will be content with these" (1 Tim. 6:6–8). Proverbs 13:25 states: "A righteous man eats until he is satisfied, but the stomach of the wicked is empty." The wicked man will never be filled no matter how much of life he consumes because he is always wanting more. Contentment comes when man loses his passion for the material and sees the primacy of the spiritual.

This is a whole new way of looking at life. I realize that. But whether spiritually speaking or practically speaking, this is God's pathway to joy, success, and genuine satisfaction in life. To see our possessions as tools with which to join him in kingdom activity rather than to fritter them away on temporary, satiable desires yields a freedom that is impossible to rival. And once experienced, it is all we'll ever want!

Caring for the Needy

Instruct them to do good, to be rich in good works,
to be generous, willing to share.

1 Timothy 6:18

My first full-time pastorate was in Galax, Virginia. The church building was a beautiful brick edifice perched atop a prominent hill outside of town. Not only was this a good location for attracting new members, but it also seemed to be a magnet for those who were in need.

Several times a day someone would stop by the church asking for assistance. Some were locals, but most were people "just driving through." We attempted to respond with love and assistance in every instance. But in my conversations with other local pastors, I discovered that many people who had received help from our church had also stopped at other churches with the same or a similar appeal.

What to do? You've thought the same thing before, I'm sure.

It was clear that some of those claiming to have a need were taking advantage of the system. We found it easy to become jaundiced in our view of the poor and just do nothing. But would the clear teaching of Scripture allow us to do that and continue to claim to be followers of Christ? In short time we were able to put into place a community-wide system that allowed us to meet genuine needs without wasting God-given resources.

What does the Bible say about this? And how can you personally—and your church family corporately—remain obedient to the heart of God as it relates to the poor?

The Old Testament Pattern

In the book of Deuteronomy, we find the fundamentals for the conduct of life among God's covenant people. In chapter 14 they were told to set aside a tenth of the produce grown in their fields as a way of providing for those who had need. (We'll look at the principle of the tithe in greater detail later.)

At the end of every three years, the people were to bring an additional tithe. "Then the Levite, who has no portion or inheritance among you, the foreign resident, fatherless, and widow within your gates, may come, eat, and be satisfied. And the LORD your God will bless you in all the work of your hands that you do" (v. 29).

In chapter 15 we discover that Israel was commanded to obey a seventh or Sabbath year where debts were to be canceled. If you read this in its entire context, you will again notice that the focus is still on the poor (v. 4). God's people were instructed to lend to the poor with a generous spirit, "to open your hand to him and freely loan him enough for whatever need he has" (v. 8). They were also instructed to cancel this debt during the Sabbath year (v. 9).

So the Lord's instructions were specific and clear: "Give to him, and don't have a stingy heart when you give, and because of this the LORD your God will bless you in all your work and in everything you do" (v. 10). He ended with a reminder that there would never cease to be poor people in the land (v. 11), and thus they were to open their hands and hearts to them freely.

The Israelites were prohibited by law from exploiting or oppressing the poor by making excessive profit off the money lent to them or withholding their wages for an unduly long time (Deut. 24:10–15). Landowners were instructed to leave grain, olives, and grapes in the fields for the poor (Lev. 19:9–10; Deut. 24:19). They were to let the land lie fallow during the seventh year so that the uncultivated land would continue to produce and the poor could be given the first right to its fruits (Exod. 23:11; Lev. 25:6).

Many of the prophets reproved Israel for ignoring the poor. Perhaps most graphic in his condemnation was Amos, a prophet from Judah who ministered in Israel about 750 BC. Amos was a layman who disclaimed professional status (7:14–15). He prophesied during a time of relative peace and prosperity but one of moral bankruptcy.

The Israelite culture of Amos's day had experienced the inevitable decay that always follows misunderstood and misdirected prosperity. Therefore, he spoke of rampant luxury and self-indulgence (1:6ff; 4:1ff; 5:10ff; 6:1ff; 8:4ff), for in spite of their prosperity, there was also great poverty among God's people and even exploitation of the poor by the wealthy.

He saved his strongest words of condemnation for women who encouraged the injustice and violence of their husbands. He called them "cows of Bashan." Our equivalent of this would be a term like "fat cows." Amos decried the way they "oppress the poor and crush the needy, who say to their husbands, 'Bring us something to drink'" (4:1). In truth the husbands didn't come off as being too sterling in this indictment either.

In chapter 5 the prophet sang a lament of judgment for a house that has fallen never to rise again, of gross injustice and reckless exploitation of the poor. "Therefore, because you trample on the poor and exact a grain tax from him, you will never live in the houses of cut stone you have built; you will never drink the wine from the lush vineyard you have planted" (5:11). Israel had taken God's blessings for granted and had ignored his commandments. In other words, they had *consumed* God's blessings and had not *conveyed* them.

Ezekiel the prophet compared Israel to her sister Sodom. "Now this was the iniquity of your sister Sodom: she and her daughters had pride, plenty of food, comfortable security, but didn't support the poor and needy" (16:49). In the famous passage where God is seen as seeking for a man to stand in the gap for him (22:30), the context suggests his concern for the poor. "The people of the land have practiced extortion and committed robbery. They have oppressed the poor and needy and unlawfully exploited the foreign resident" (22:29).

Solomon made a clear connection between serving the poor and honoring God. "The one who oppresses the poor insults their Maker, but one who is kind to the needy honors Him" (Prov. 14:31; cp. 17:5). We looked at Psalm 72 yesterday as we discussed God's desire to provide abundantly for our own needs. I would recommend that you read this psalm in its entirety. In verse 3 Solomon prays for prosperity, and in verse 4 he gives the reason. "May he vindicate the afflicted among the people, help the poor; and crush the oppressor." Look down at verses 12–13: "For he will rescue the poor who cry out and the afflicted who have no helper. He will have pity on the poor who cry out and the afflicted who have no helper. He will have pity on the poor and helpless and save the lives of the poor. He will redeem them from oppression and violence, for their lives are precious in his sight."

The clear message of the Old Testament is that God's heart beats for the poor, that he reaches out to meet their need, and that his preferred way of doing so is to meet their need through us—so that the needs of both of us can be met at the same time.

The Ministry of Jesus

Jesus initiated his ministry with this declaration taken from the prophet Isaiah: "The Spirit of the Lord is on Me, because He has anointed Me to preach good news to the poor" (Luke 4:18a). When John the Baptist sent his disciples to ask if Jesus was the promised one, Jesus told them to tell John what they had seen, how he had healed the sick and preached the gospel to the poor (Matt. 11:5).

When we look at Jesus' ministry, we see that he manifested the Father's concern for the disadvantaged. He cared for lepers and outcasts. He healed the widow's son, exhibiting concern for her situation.

Tragically, some who are constantly looking for ways to avoid the obvious teaching of Scripture have misapplied one event in Jesus' ministry to provide an excuse for not caring for the poor. We have memorialized this story with the lovely song, "Broken and Spilled Out," about a woman so moved by love that she poured expensive oil on Jesus' head. The disciples were indignant at the apparent waste (Matt. 26:8). They suggested the oil could have been sold for a great deal of money and given to the poor, to which Jesus responded, "You always have the poor with you, but you do not always have Me" (v. 11).

John, in his Gospel, told us that Judas Iscariot was the disciple who most strenuously objected to such waste (not exactly the kind of person we want to model our theology after). Further, John gives us insight as to why Judas was so concerned about her "wasteful" generosity. "He didn't say this because he cared about the poor but because he was a thief" (12:6). This woman's gift of worship had deprived him of money he could have pilfered for his own gain. The love of money is indeed an insidious evil. Look at Judas for one telling example.

If we look at the text on its face value, Jesus' statement about the ever-presence of the poor clearly reflects the concern echoed in Deuteronomy 15:11. In both instances the obvious concern is not that we are therefore given the right to ignore them but that we must do all we can to join the Father in meeting their needs. A similar assumption is behind Jesus' statement in Matthew 6:2: "So whenever you give to the poor, don't sound a trumpet before you." Jesus anticipated that we would give to the poor. He simply wanted our motive for giving to be as generous as our gift.

Caring for the poor and needy is a kingdom activity done for the glory of the King who himself will reward the giver (Matt. 6:4).

The story of Zacchaeus provides us an example of a man who experienced true conversion. He was a tax collector who had become rich by taking advantage of the poor. But when Jesus invited himself to Zacchaeus's house, this man of ill-gotten means responded, "Look, I'll give half of my possession to the poor, Lord! And if I have extorted anything from anyone, I'll pay back four times as much!" (Luke 19:8). Jesus declared, "Today salvation has come to this house" (19:9). This passage does not teach "works salvation" but points to the truth that salvation will bring about a radical transformation in how we view money and the poor.

The Early Church

Those who continued following Jesus after his death, resurrection, and ascension into glory maintained this well-established practice of having godly concern for the poor.

Few stories thrill me like that of the rapid advance of the early church. I long to see the day when we will experience three thousand baptisms daily. When we look at that early church community, we often rightly draw attention to their emphasis on apostolic teaching, fellowship, prayer, and evangelism. But we should not neglect their concern for the needy, how "they sold their possessions and property and distributed the proceeds to all, as anyone had a need" (Acts 2:45). This text does not suggest communal living but rather indicates a community of generosity.

Caring for the needy was such a critical function of the early church that we are reminded in Acts 4 about this ministry, with the bold emphasis that there was not a needy person to be found among them (4:34). Imagine that! The context suggests that they had developed a system for caring for the needy. When someone sold a possession, they brought the proceeds and laid them at the apostles' feet for distribution. The enlargement of the ministry team through the selection of "deacons" was also prompted by the growth of the church and the accompanying need to care for the widows (Acts 6).

We find this pattern of generosity toward the needy being continued by the church at Antioch (Acts 11). Theirs was a vibrant, growing fellowship of faith. Twice we are told about the large numerical increase in this church (vv. 21, 24). When a team of prophets came from Jerusalem, informing the believers there about an impending famine that would impact the Roman world, the response of the church in Antioch was immediate and generous. "Each of the disciples, according to his ability, determined to send relief to the brothers who lived in Judea" (v. 29).

It appears that this famine relief offering spread throughout all the known churches. In writing to the Romans, Paul noted, "For Macedonia and Achaia were pleased to make a contribution to the poor among the saints in Jerusalem" (Rom. 15:26). Second Corinthians 8 and 9, two chapters we will look at in greater detail later on, were aimed at encouraging the church at Antioch to complete their offering, their ministry of service which was "supplying the needs of the saints" (9:12).

New Testament teaching throughout indicates that meeting the needs of the less fortunate is an appropriate use of kingdom resources. We are not surprised to read in Ephesians 4:28 that Paul exhorted the thief to quit stealing and get an honest job. But why? The end result is somewhat surprising—"so that he has something to share with anyone in need."

In 1 Timothy 6:17, Paul told those who had ample and abundant resources to be rich in good works, generous, and willing to share. He likewise concluded the book of Titus with the appeal, "And our people must also learn to devote themselves to good works for cases of urgent need, so they will not be unfruitful (3:14). James declared that pure and undefiled religion requires that we "look after orphans and widows" and keep ourselves "unstained by the world" (1:27).

Thus, we see that a vital use of God's resources, which have been given to us in sacred trust, is to care for those with physical needs. This is demanded both individually and corporately.

The local church must think strategically about this task. We are challenged to assist each other in providing a means whereby our cooperative efforts allow us to make a far greater impact on others than any individual can by working alone.

Do you think it would be possible for your church, working with other like-minded churches, to actually eradicate need in your community? Do you think God is able to make sufficient resources available?

What if Christians worldwide began to work together to deal with the issues that cause poverty? What if we all began to give a cup of water in his name, to seek to meet both the physical and spiritual needs of those around us?

What if we were to give the thirsty water and introduce them to the Living Water?

What if we were to give them bread and also show them the Bread of Life?

I believe such ministry-based evangelism is one of the tools the King has provided to enable us to complete the Acts 1:8 assignment of being witnesses here and "to the ends of the earth."

Week 2, Day 4

Ministry Support and Expansion

Then the people rejoiced because of their leaders' willingness to give, for they had given to the LORD with a whole heart. King David also rejoiced greatly.

1 CHRONICLES 29:9

God has given me so many learning opportunities that I am humbled to consider how good he has been to me. When I was just thirty-two years old, I went to pastor First Baptist Church in Norfolk, Virginia. God was gracious to give us accelerated growth. This soon led to the opportunity to provide additional space for meeting the needs of the expanding population of the Hampton Roads area. Our greatest need was for a preschool and children's building.

As pastor I needed to set an example of joyous, sacrificial giving. But we had a challenge. My wife had just given birth to our third daughter. So we now had three children at home, the oldest being eight.

What was I to give, and how would I manage?

This was the first time I had ever really struggled with giving. My dad was a Baptist preacher, and tithing had never really been an option or an issue with me. It was just a way of life. But now I had to make a volitional decision about how to participate in providing for the building of a new facility for our ministry.

God used this event mightily to teach me about joyous giving and about his ability to provide for all our needs. And you know what I learned through that process and season of our lives? I learned that the expansion of ministry is one of the purposes for which God provides resources.

We will always have what we need to give.

Buildings of Ministry

The Bible gives us several good examples of what to expect of building ministries. We have probably all experienced this at one time or another in our individual churches, a time when we sensed the Lord calling us to grow and expand our facilities to reach more people and to minister more effectively. This does have biblical precedent.

THE TABERNACLE

God had delivered Israel from Egyptian slavery and brought them to himself in the wilderness. He had given them the laws by which they would live in covenant relationship with him, and now he instructed Moses, "Tell the Israelites to take an offering for Me. You are to take My offering from everyone whose heart stirs him to give" (Exod. 25:2).

This passage serves as an introduction, then, explaining the source of the materials that were to be used later for the construction of the tent of meeting, the tabernacle. And its purpose was made explicitly clear in Exodus 25:8: "They are to make a sanctuary for Me so that I may dwell among them." It was to be a constant reminder of the presence of the Lord.

This was a unique aspect of Israel's religion and of Israel's God, that he dwelled among his people. He was not a regional god, constricted to the confines of any geographic region. No matter where they traveled, he would be in their midst. The tabernacle thus provided a visible reminder of his presence. It was a place for them to worship and serve their God.

But notice that the giving that preceded its construction was *voluntary*. The grace of God alone would be the motivation that would stir their hearts to give. Israel understood that God had brought them from bondage into freedom, from death unto life, and thus they were moved to give their greatest treasures to provide for this place of worship.

In Exodus 35 we pick up the story of the building of the tabernacle. In verse 5 we are reminded again that the offering was to come from a willing heart, not just the offering of money but also of time and of talent.

Those with various skills put those skills to use in the construction of the tabernacle.

And throughout the building process, "the people continued to bring freewill offerings morning after morning" (Exod. 36:3). In fact, the craftsmen told Moses that the people were bringing *too much*, more than they even needed. Moses had to send a proclamation throughout the land: "Let no man or woman make anything else as an offering for the sanctuary" (v. 6). I love the last statement in this section: "There was more than enough" (v. 7).

When people begin responding to God's heartbeat, there will be more than enough! God will make available through us the resources necessary to advance his kingdom. He certainly did so in the building of the tabernacle.

THE TEMPLE

After the Promised Land was inhabited, God gave David a burden to build a permanent place of worship. He struggled with the knowledge that he was living in a house of cedar while the ark of God sat inside tent curtains (2 Sam. 7:2). Through Nathan the prophet, God told David that the task of building the temple would not be his but would instead be given to his son Solomon (v. 13).

David could have been disappointed by this news, but instead he broke into a prayer of praise and thanksgiving, heralding God's goodness (vv. 18–29). David's motivation for building the temple was clearly focused on God's name and his reign, not on whether it would be accomplished on David's timetable or even in his lifetime. "Do as you have promised," he said to the Lord, "so that Your name will be exalted forever" (vv. 25b–26a).

We are given even greater insight into the depth and motivation for David's generosity in 1 Chronicles 29:1–2. He recognized that Solomon was young and inexperienced and that the task set before him was immense. The temple was to be a palatial structure to remind the people that the true King of Israel was the Lord God himself! He specifically noted, "The temple will not be for man, but for the LORD God."

Therefore, David gave toward this project to the best of his ability. His generosity is detailed in verses 2–5. He gave from his own personal treasures, over and above all that he had provided for the "holy house" (v. 3)—probably a reference to his regular support required through the giving of the tithe. He then challenged others to follow his example. The verb translated "volunteer" (v. 5) is used elsewhere in reference to making freewill offerings for the building of the tabernacle (Exod. 25:2; 35:21, 29) and for the second temple (Ezra. 1:6). David viewed these gifts as symbols of Israel's giving themselves to the Lord as a kingdom of priests.

Before we leave this passage, we should also note the impact of this generous giving for the building of the temple. "Then the people rejoiced because of their leaders' willingness to give, for they had given to the LORD with a whole heart. King David also rejoiced greatly" (1 Chron. 29:9).

What produces that kind of joy in giving?

The present text makes it abundantly clear. I recommend, in fact, that you read David's prayer in its entirety (vv. 10–19). In verse 11, he notes that everything in the heavens and on earth belongs to the Lord, that "Yours, LORD, is the kingdom, and You are exalted as head over all."

So here's the bottom line: "LORD our God, all this wealth that we've provided for building You a house for Your holy name comes from Your hand; everything belongs to You" (v. 16).

We are told, "They ate and drank with great joy in the LORD's presence that day" (v. 22). Why? Why such a theme of joy?

Because it is the nature of God to give. Thus when God's people give, they are responding to his nature that dwells within them. When we behave like our Father, it always produces joy.

This is a consistent theme of Scripture. In the days of Nehemiah, the people gave to rebuild the city wall. Listen to the refrain: "On that day they offered great sacrifices and rejoiced because God had given them great joy. The women and children also celebrated, and Jerusalem's rejoicing was heard far away" (Neh. 12:43).

Both the tabernacle and the temple were built with resources God had supplied his people.

THE CHEST OF JOASH

No, God's people did not suddenly begin meeting in a wooden trunk, but this important object lesson—the chest of Joash—had a great deal to do with the future of the temple and its resurgence as a place of worship.

Joash came to the throne of Israel at a time when pagan worship had been tolerated and the temple had fallen into great disrepair. It was now over a century old.

Joash clearly desired a spiritual change in the people's hearts, a commitment that is best illustrated in his desire to repair the temple (2 Kings 12:1–16). So he instructed the priests to take all the dedicated money brought to the temple, as well as all the money that had been voluntarily given, and to use it in repairing the damages to the temple.

Later, however, Joash discovered that the repairs had not been made (v. 6), and he held the priests accountable. So he instructed Jehoiada the priest to build a collection box, allowing the people a central location where they could give money for the repair of the temple.

Second Chronicles 24:9–11 tells us that the box's presence and purpose was broadcast throughout the land. We read the text and marvel at the spontaneous response: "All the leaders and all the people rejoiced, brought the tax, and put it in the chest until it was full" (v. 10). The Chronicler tells us, "They did this daily and gathered money in abundance" (v. 11). And when the repair was finished, they gave the overage to the king to provide for articles for ministry (v. 14).

We should consider it a privilege when God gives us the opportunity to invest his resources in the provision of buildings that enable us to make his name known by advancing his kingdom. We must also be responsible to ensure that our purpose in building is consistent with his kingdom's purposes, not dictated by our ego or convenience. We should also never take from the funds necessary to proclaim the gospel to the nations, redirecting them into the construction of facilities, for God possesses sufficient resources for us to give freely beyond that which is necessary for ministry concerns.

Building Support

Beyond brick and mortar, however, God also allows his people the privilege of providing resources for those individuals who are engaged in ministry. Too often we can become so focused on buildings that we lose sight of the fact that they are nothing more than a wrapper that goes around the work of ministry. Our greatest opportunity to invest in God's kingdom is to invest in those who are giving their lives for the ministry.

THE OLD TESTAMENT PATTERN

In Deuteronomy 18, God laid out a pattern by which Israel was allowed to support those who were ministers of God. The priests, in common with the whole tribe of Levi, had no inheritance in Israel (v. 2 and cp. 10:9). But they had been chosen by the Lord to minister in his name (v. 5) and therefore deserved to be supported from specified portions of the offerings that were given to God.

The book of Numbers details the story of Israel preparing to enter the land of promise. Many of the principles taught earlier are restated here in preparation for a more settled existence. In chapter 18, for example, the Lord spoke to Aaron about the responsibility he and his sons would have for the sanctuary. Further, he instructed Aaron to include the tribe of Levi, who would join them in ministry at the tent of meeting (v. 3).

The Levites were not given a tribal inheritance in the Promised Land but were placed instead into forty-eight Levitical cities spread throughout the land (Num. 35:1–8). During the wilderness journey they had been responsible for setting up, dismantling, and transporting the tabernacle, as well as conducting worship (Num. 1:47–54 and 3:14–39), assisting the priests by preparing the offerings, purifying the instruments, and singing praise, while the priestly family of Aaron fulfilled their duties of offering the sacrifices in the tabernacle (Exod. 28; Lev. 8–10).

Both the priests and the Levites were consecrated to God. They were his gift to Israel in order to perform duties of worship. Because of their ministry, the holiness of both the tabernacle and the temple were maintained, and the presence of God dwelt among Israel.

And since the Levites and priests had given themselves to God and his ministry, a portion of the tithe from the rest of the nation was to be used to provide for their needs. Families were also encouraged to invite the Levites to join them in eating and the celebration of national feasts (Deut. 12:12, 18).

So here in Numbers 18, the Lord told Aaron that all the offerings of the Israelites would be brought to the priests (v. 8) and that a portion of those offerings were to be kept by the priests (v. 9) and the Levites (v. 21). The fact that the Levites were told to give a tenth of the tenth they received (v. 26) indicates that their livelihood was being provided through the gifts of the people of Israel.

Therefore, the generous support of the people of God enabled those involved in ministry to dedicate themselves fully rather than being concerned about earning a living. That is the Old Testament pattern.

THE PATTERN OF JESUS

When Jesus sent out the twelve disciples, he instructed them; "Don't take a traveling bag for the road, or an extra shirt, sandals, or a walking stick, for the worker is worthy of his food" (Matt. 10:10; cp. Mark 6:8–11). Jesus' instructions underlined not only the urgency and significance of this ministry but also the fact that those on mission are to leave the provision for their ministry to the Lord. This is not a call to asceticism but an assurance that God will make provision through the generosity of those to whom they minister.

The statement that the "worker is worthy of his food" is an affirmation of the value of ministry, and it is an encouragement to us to participate in that ministry by supporting the workers who come our way.

This statement of implicit support in no wise contradicts the statement in verse 8b: "You have received free of charge; give free of charge." These followers of Jesus were not like the mercenary prophets who became a plague to the church by the end of the first century (Didache 11–12). The true Christian worker can never be "hired," but his work is so vital he deserves to be supported.

THE PRACTICE OF THE EARLY CHURCH

Among the earliest letters written by the apostle Paul were 1 Thessalonians and Galatians. They give us a glimpse at the developing structure of ministry in the early church.

In 1 Thessalonians, Paul did not speak about providing financial resources for those in ministry, but he did establish an important principle concerning the relationship between the brothers and those who labor among them. The members of the church at Thessalonica were exhorted to "esteem them very highly in love because of their work" (1 Thess. 5:13). In other words, the love relationship between our ministry leaders and us should be based on the great value of our work together. With kingdom activity at stake, we cannot allow petty prejudices to cloud our vision.

In Galatians 6, Paul gave some practical guidelines for life in the Christian community. He envisioned a healthy fellowship where restoration of the fallen and the sharing of burdens would be the norm (vv. 1–2). He anticipated that every member of the community would have some area of ministry and that each person would be required to "carry his own load" (vv. 4–5).

But then he gave specific instruction about caring for those who teach the Word. "The one who is taught the message must share his goods with the teacher" (v. 6).

Apparently, some form of organized system existed in the local church that enabled people to recognize those who were appointed to teach and minister the Word and also obligated the church to provide them financial support. This is actually implied in Acts 6, where servants (or deacons) were appointed to ensure that the apostles had sufficient time to devote themselves to the ministries of prayer and teaching. Indeed, the "goods" mentioned in Galatians 6 do refer to worldly wealth, just as in the story of the rich young ruler (Luke 12:18). While no specific amount is indicated, it is clear that the support should be sufficient to provide a standard of living commensurate with the high and holy calling of ministry.

The subsequent statement—"Don't be deceived: God is not mocked" (Gal. 6:7)—also grabs our attention. We often quote this phrase but with little regard for its context. Paul was saying in the strongest possible terms that the believer cannot ignore this instruction of God.

It is not unusual for Paul to use "giving" and "sowing" together in the same context (cp. 2 Cor. 9:6). But in this case Paul was warning that those who failed to care for their teachers were sowing to the flesh and not the Spirit. It would be sheer hypocrisy to claim to be a kingdom-minded person and not support those who are giving their life to ministry. Giving to those who serve God as a vocation gives us double joy—the joy of obedience to our Father and the joy of investment in his kingdom.

Paul wrote to the Corinthians about his own apostolic work among them. Using himself as an example, he asked about his right to refrain from working while serving them in the Lord (1 Cor. 9:6). He then gave several examples to fortify his point—the soldier who stops his normal duties to go to war, the worker in the vineyard who is entitled to eat of its fruit, the shepherds who drink the milk of the flock. He even quoted from the law: "For it is written in the Law of Moses, Do not muzzle an ox while it treads out the grain" (v. 9).

To ensure that the Corinthians did not miss the obvious point of his illustrations, he added, "If we have sown spiritual things for you, is it too much if we reap material things from you?" (v. 11). He ended his argument with an appeal to the highest possible authority: "In the same way, the Lord has commanded that those who preach the gospel should earn their living by the gospel (v. 14).

On certain occasions Paul waived his right to receive support from the church and chose instead to work as a tent maker. He did so, however—in one case—so as not to become a burden to the young church at Thessalonica (1 Thess. 2:9) and because he was already being supported by the Philippian church (Phil. 4:16). The other instance was in Corinth where he did so because of the spiritual immaturity of the believers there (1 Cor. 9:15).

Paul in his first letter to Timothy indicated that the support of those in ministry should be generous. "The elders who are good leaders should be considered worthy of an ample honorarium, especially those who work hard at preaching and teaching" (5:17). Some translations read "double honor." The context leaves little doubt that Paul had in mind generous financial remuneration.

It is tragic to see a church try to "hire" a pastor or staff member at a bargain price and then suggest that this person is not very spiritual because he can't feed his family on a subsistence salary. Some want their pastor or staff to live "by faith" even though the people who make up the church itself are unwilling to do so. The truth is, the "by faith" part of that equation should be the faith of the church members to believe that God has enough resources to enable them to provide for those in ministry.

Some estimate that nearly 80 percent of evangelical churches in America are on a plateau or declining. Is it any wonder that many of our churches stand under the judgment of God, who has warned us that he will not be mocked and that we will in time reap what we sow.

God has given us ample resources to provide for our needs and pleasures, to assist those in need, and to provide a living for those who are devoting their lives for kingdom advance.

All of it is there. But where is it when it counts?

Reaching the Nations

May his name endure forever; as long as the sun shines, may his fame increase. May all nations be blessed by him and call him blessed.

PSALM 72:17

A few years ago when I was given the opportunity to lead an emphasis called Empowering Kingdom Growth, I undertook a study on the concept of the kingdom. And throughout my time of study and writing, I was overwhelmed by the repeated biblical refrain—"the nations."

I am certainly not the only person or the first person to see this, to recognize that God's heartbeat is for all the nations on Earth to know him. In truth, I sometimes wonder why it took *me* so long to see that it runs like a golden strand throughout the Bible.

If God is intent that all the nations be blessed by him and call him blessed, does it not follow that he would make available the resources to accomplish this great mission venture?

That's why another kingdom theme that runs throughout the Scripture is God's desire to bless those who will *embody his name, embrace his mission* to the nations, and *obey his word.* I believe the Scripture teaches that God desires to provide all the resources needed to accomplish his stated purpose of reaching the nations. He is still looking for individuals, churches, and denominational groups who will dare to take his Word seriously and join him in this task.

The Reciprocal Nature of Blessing

Genesis 11 recounts the attempt of man to make a name for himself by building a tower to the heavens (11:5). This led, of course, to the scattering of the nations and the confusion of differing languages.

The story of the redemption of the nations, however—like that of creation—began with God speaking (Gen. 12:1). The call to Abram to forsake everything and follow God is reminiscent of the call of the disciples in the New Testament. It is startling to note that Abram was not given a destination but only a promise. Every great faith journey begins in precisely this same way.

At this point in your life, in fact, you may be wondering where God is leading you. I encourage you to relax and enjoy the journey, for the promise of God is sure and his presence is sufficient. Guaranteed.

His promises to Abram, for example, were not to be fulfilled immediately but at some time in the future, once again indicating that faith is always required in our spiritual pilgrimage. "I will make you into a great nation," the Lord said to him. "I will bless you, I will make your name great. . . . I will bless those who bless you, I will curse those who treat you with contempt" (vv. 2–3). God's blessing always involves his promised presence, provision, and protection. We need to learn this significant truth.

We sometimes miss the reciprocal nature of blessing. The second half of verse 2—"you will be a blessing"—and the last half of verse three—"all the peoples on earth will be blessed through you" make clear that Abram was blessed that he might impart blessing.

Blessing for all the nations was God's vision that many in Israel failed to comprehend or embrace. The patriarchal period ended with Israel in Egypt, seeking resources God had promised to them if they would be a blessing to the peoples of the earth.

Essentially, they had consumed God's blessings and had not conveyed them. There is a succinct reminder of this global theme in Exodus 19:5–6, which reappears in the Psalms and in the prophets. But by and large, it never became an intentional and consistent strategy for Israel. Only when the King himself established a community of believers to whom he imparted his own Spirit with the commission to go to the ends of the earth did this role return with intentionality and purpose.

Fill the Earth with Glory

Psalm 72 was likely written to celebrate an anniversary of Solomon's accession to the throne. It presents the ideals of kingship that Solomon's prayer at Gibeon expressed so well (1 Kings 3:6–9). Righteousness dominates the opening section of the psalm, but the theme of extravagant abundance is always near the surface.

As you read the psalm for yourself, you may find it sounding more familiar than usual since we looked at it earlier in our focus on the poor and underprivileged. We're looking at it again now to notice its focus on the nations.

In verse 5, we encounter a prayer for an endless reign. "May he continue while the sun endures, and as long as the moon, throughout all generations." This theme is repeated in verse 7—"until the moon is no more"— and again in verse 17—"as long as the sun shines." It's not difficult to see that these verses look beyond an earthly king and point to the eternal King (cp. John 12:34).

The psalmist prays that his rule will extend from sea to sea and to the ends of the earth (v. 8). "Sea to sea" may have in mind the promised boundaries in Exodus 23:31—"I will set your borders from the Red Sea to the Mediterranean Sea, and from the wilderness to the Euphrates River."

The bottom line: "Let all kings bow down to him, all nations serve him" (Ps. 72:11).

He envisioned that the kings of Tarshish and the coasts and islands would bring tribute. Verse 10 mentions the gifts of tributes from the kings of Sheba and Seba. You may recall that the Queen of Sheba was one of many who brought gifts to Solomon (1 Kings 10:1ff.). But the psalmist looked beyond these gifts of courtesy to gifts of total homage to the eternal King, of abundant and endless blessing.

Several kinds of wealth are mentioned—gold (v. 15) and an abundance of grain (v. 16). He saw the people flourishing in the cities like the grass of the field (v. 16). The terms of verse 17 are virtually those of the promise to Abram.

But why is all this abundance desired?

Solomon delivers the answer in the form of a prayer: "May all nations be blessed by him and call him blessed."

God's passion is for all the nations to relate to him as rightful King. It is therefore not surprising that he desires for his resources to be used for that end. Further, it is abundantly clear that he has created the world and endowed it with sufficient resources to accomplish this task.

So we must ask ourselves, "Why then has this task not been completed?" The answer must lie in our failure to obey his directions concerning the accumulation and disposition of his resources.

Let the Nations Know

If you have read *Empowering Kingdom Growth* and participated in the accompanying forty-day study, you will be familiar with Ezekiel 36. Israel was in Babylonian captivity. Essentially they had *consumed* God's blessings and had not *conveyed* them. They had ignored his concern for the nations.

But the prophet not only told them why they had suffered the ignominy of captivity. He also looked beyond this dark chapter to a day of restoration. God planned to honor his name by manifesting his holiness through his people in the sight of the nations. He promised that he would give his people a new heart and would place his Spirit within them (vv. 26–27). He illustrated the Spirit's animating power by the vision of the valley of dry bones where the breath entered the bones and they stood to their feet, a mighty army (37:9–10).

The prophet used several pictures of abundance. He spoke of summoning the grain and making it plentiful (v. 29), of the fruit trees producing in abundance (v. 30), of the barren land becoming like the garden of Eden (v. 35), of desolate cities being inhabited and fortified (v. 35) and the number of people being multiplied (v. 38).

Again, why would God bestow such extravagant abundance? The last phrase of verse 38 puts everything in bold perspective—"Then they will know that I am the LORD." The context makes clear that God provides these abundant resources for the reaching of the nations.

All Authority, All Nations

Finally, we go into the New Testament, where we find the disciples stunned by the rapid events that had taken their King away from Earth and back into heaven. But in thinking back to their last moments with him on Earth, one statement begins to resonate with meaning and purpose.

In obedience they had proceeded to the mountain where Jesus had told them to meet him (Matt. 28:16). Anxiety and uncertainty had collided with joy and worship (v. 17), and to quell their fear Jesus had come near and spoken to them.

His ringing declaration, "All authority has been given to Me in heaven and on earth" (v. 18), must have been reassuring. This magnificent declaration is given deeper significance when one understands that it is based on the promise of Daniel 7:14— "He was given authority to rule, and glory, and a kingdom; so that those of every people, nation, and language should serve Him. His dominion is an everlasting dominion that will not pass away, and His kingdom is one that will not be destroyed."

Jesus had authority during his earthly ministry (Matt. 7:29). But on the hillside that day, he declared that he had been given "all authority." At the beginning of his ministry, Satan had offered him all the kingdoms of the world and their glory (Matt. 4:8–9), but now through obedience and suffering, he had been given all authority "in heaven and on earth."

The implication of "all authority" is not difficult to understand. He has been given everything necessary to complete the kingdom task assigned by his Father—the reaching of the nations.

It is not surprising that the mention of "all authority" is followed by a comprehensive and universal mission—"all nations." Membership in the new kingdom community is not based on race but on relationship, and therefore Jesus described the mission in terms of making "disciples." "Going," "baptizing," and "teaching" are participles that further define the singular imperative—"make disciples."

Jesus, through his death and resurrection, has made possible the completion of the task assigned by the Father—the reaching of the nations. And this is why it is puzzling to think that the church has made such little headway in accomplishing this task, especially when we understand that God has made all resources available to the church for this mission.

Could it be that we have ignored both the mission and the means? Many believers are struggling with their personal finances, and their church community is struggling for survival rather than moving aggressively ahead to reach the nations.

It is time for us to take a fresh look at how God desires to make his resources available. Next week we will look at God's directions on how to earn money, overcome debt, spend it, and give it with kingdom purpose.

Earning, Spending, Saving, Investing

Whole-Life Stewardship

*Why does a fool have money in his hand
with no intention of buying wisdom?*

PROVERBS 17:16

Solomon, the author of many of the Proverbs, certainly embodied the sentiment of the featured verse above. When he was chosen to be king, he traveled to Gibeon to offer sacrifice to the Lord. In response the Lord appeared to him in a dream and said, "Ask. What should I give you?" (1 Kings 3:5).

How would you have responded to that question? Be honest! What would have been the first thing to enter your mind?

As Solomon began to answer, he admitted that he was young and inexperienced as a leader (v. 7) and that the task before him was overwhelming (v. 8). Thus he asked for an obedient heart and for the ability to discern between good and evil (v. 9). In other words, he asked for the wisdom to know the heart of God and for the willingness to obey it.

He bought wisdom!

Solomon's request greatly pleased the Lord. He had not asked for long life, riches for himself, or victory over his enemies—requests that may have been appropriate for a king. Thus God declared that he would grant Solomon's request for wisdom and in addition would give him riches and honor (v. 11). Solomon, in return, would be required to walk in God's ways and obey his Word.

How do you want to respond to God's question, "What should I give you?" The fact that you are engaged in this study suggests that you are seeking wisdom and the willingness to obey. You're off to a good start, but let me warn you that the adversary will attempt to use your old nature to lure you into rebellion against the wisdom contained in God's Word. The drama of the garden is repeated in all of our lives. Satan wants you to doubt God's good intention.

Remember these basics, which we've touched on before:

God is the Creator and owner of all that exists. "The earth and everything in it, the world and its inhabitants, belong to the LORD" (Ps. 24:1). You must affirm this not just with your mouth and your head but with your heart. This truth must begin to influence every decision you make concerning your life. Think about this—the Creator is the only one who fully understands how his creation works! Thus to ask him for discernment and for the willingness to obey what he reveals is to *buy wisdom.*

God created us in his image. This means that we are *rational, responsible, and relational.* We are unique in his creation and have been given the privilege and responsibility for the management of all his resources. Therefore, we are *stewards* and not *owners.* And because every steward will be held accountable for his stewardship, it is critical that we buy wisdom—the biblical principles for the management of life.

Material possessions are equally irrelevant at both our entrance into the world and our exit from it. "For we brought nothing into the world, and we can take nothing out" (1 Tim. 6:7). We've already considered the parable of the man who ignored this truth and responded to his God-given abundance by hoarding it, only to be judged because he stored up treasures for himself on earth but was not rich toward God (Luke 12:13–21). He didn't choose to *buy wisdom* with his wealth.

Material possessions have meaning when we use them according to God's intention. He graciously allows us to use them for our needs and pleasures but also to care for the needy, to invest in ministry, and to advance his kingdom. What he wants is for these also to become our pleasure, our delight. When you look at your budget, does it reflect God's priorities? Or does it reflect your need to buy wisdom?

God desires to provide additional resources to those who are committed to kingdom principles. This includes the earning, spending, investing, and giving of his resources. This is easy for a parent to understand. We know it is our responsibility to provide for our children, but this task becomes a pleasure when we see them using these resources responsibly as well, not merely when we're doing it for them. Isn't this the principle at work in the promise, "Give, and it will be given to you; a good measure—pressed down, shaken together, and running over—will be poured into your lap" (Luke 6:38)? The parable of the talents confirms God's desire to provide additional resources to those who are faithful servants, who know what it means to forsake the fakes and *buy wisdom*.

But be assured that the adversary will oppose you at every turn. His goal is to advance his kingdom and thwart that of the rightful King. Thus we must expect opposition when our heart is set on *buying wisdom*.

All of Me

When you read a Christian book on money or hear a sermon on stewardship, do you ever think, *All they want is my money?* I suppose we all have! That's the old nature crying out.

First, it's not really *my* money, is it? And second, God is not dependent on "my resources" to reach the world. He owns the cattle on a thousand hills. He is, however, concerned about me and about you. He wants us to enjoy the great privilege of joining him in advancing his kingdom on Earth.

Anytime we think about stewardship, we must think of it in terms of totality—whole life. How can I use my workplace as a forum for kingdom advance? How should I conduct my business so that it reflects his character? How should we order our home so that it fosters kingdom activity?

What about suffering and affliction? Paul opened his second letter to the Corinthians talking about the stewardship of comfort. "He comforts us in all our affliction, so that we may be able to comfort those who are in any kind of affliction, through the comfort we ourselves receive from God" (2 Cor. 1:4). God wastes nothing. He can redeem everything that comes into our lives. Even the terrible things can be cashed out into expressions of understanding and comfort that bring healing into other's lives.

When it comes to money, God is not simply concerned about the tithe—the 10 percent we are required to return to him. He is concerned about 100 percent of all that he allows to flow through our lives. Thus we need to "buy wisdom" in regard to every aspect of our financial management.

Don't ever forget, you are special to God. You were created in his image, redeemed by his grace, gifted and empowered to serve alongside him for the advancement of his kingdom. It's a great assignment, and it should make us desire to *buy wisdom*.

Satan: Financial Terrorist

"A thief comes only to steal and to kill and to destroy" (John 10:10).

Do you know the context of that statement? Jesus declared himself to be the Good Shepherd, contrasting himself with thieves and hirelings. He talked about his desire that the sheep could come and go and find pasture (v. 9), how the good shepherd cares first and foremost for his sheep and is willing to lay down his life for them (v. 11). He did all of this so that we could have life and have it in abundance (v. 10b).

If we know this to be true in the spiritual realm, and we do, why do we have such great difficulty believing that the Good Shepherd desires our best in all of life, including the financial realm? Why are we more likely to listen to the world's wisdom concerning how we earn, spend, invest, and give money than we are God's? Here's why: because our adversary, the devil, is a financial terrorist who wants to destroy everything that God has created and has called "very good."

I find it interesting that two of the focal points of Satan's attack are human sexuality and financial resources. He attempts to cheapen and abuse both of these wonderful gifts of the Good Shepherd. We have thus sought to use both as instruments of personal gratification. We have bought the lie of the enemy, and we are paying the price.

Both nationally and personally, we are struggling with a staggering debt problem, and yet we so often listen to the adversary and ignore the Creator. Don't be confused: Satan is not your ally. He is at heart a financial terrorist who will use every scheme possible to keep you from *buying wisdom.*

He will whisper in your ear—"Did God really say . . . ?" He will suggest that God is withholding something good. He will entice you to unbridled consumerism. He'll whisper, "Go ahead, you deserve it." He will lure you with offers of financial gain that seem "too good to be true."

And every time we buy his lie, we will reap the consequences and discover that he desires only to destroy.

No matter how much you own, God doesn't need it to accomplish his purpose. He created your wealth in the first place, and he can remove it if he desires. But he has given it to you in trust to allow you to participate in kingdom advance.

So buy wisdom with it.

To pursue blindly a financial course without understanding God's directives, and then praying for him to rectify the results, is to court financial disaster as well as God's judgment. God will provide both discernment and the heart for obedience if you simply ask him.

How to Earn Money

What does a man gain for all his efforts
he labors at under the sun?

ECCLESIASTES 1:3

Have you ever asked yourself a question similar to the one Solomon asked at the beginning of Ecclesiastes? I must tell you that in context, it follows a pretty distressing statement: "Absolute futility," Solomon had surmised. "Everything is futile" (1:2b).

I've actually gone up to people and asked them why they go to work on Monday morning. Most openly confess that they go because they have financial necessities that force them to do so. In other words, work is simply a necessity because we need money to live.

But since much of our life is spent this way—earning a living so that we can provide for necessities and prepare for the future—it would be wise for us to examine the advice the Creator gives us concerning how we earn our money.

I taught for a year at Wingate College after I returned from England. I had one particularly bright student who was also particularly unmotivated. So I held him after class one day to ask him why he didn't apply himself any better. His response startled me. "You're forced to go to school, which you don't enjoy, to get a job that you won't like, to earn enough so you can afford to retire and enjoy yourself, but then you're too old to enjoy it, and ultimately you die." No wonder he wasn't motivated! If that was the whole story of life, then Solomon's first assessment is right—"Absolute futility!"

Here's how Solomon got there. He began a search for meaning and purpose in life, and his first conclusions about work were actually pretty depressing. He first declared, "I hated all my work at which I labored under the sun because I must leave it to the man who comes after me" (2:18). He worried that no matter how hard he labored, with no matter how much great wisdom and skill, he would still end up leaving his hard-earned resources to someone else, most likely someone who was foolish, someone who couldn't manage resources he hadn't earned himself. Listen to Solomon's despair for the workingman: "For all his days are filled with grief, and his occupation is sorrowful; even at night, his mind does not rest. This too is futile" (2:23).

But we begin to see a ray of hope as Solomon begins to discover God's principles for work.

Work in Perspective

The first real breakthrough came when Solomon acknowledged a fundamental principle of life: *God is the owner, man is the manager, and therefore man's labor is from the hand of God.* This principle is as old as the garden. God created the earth and all that is within it, and then he gave man the privilege of cultivating it as his steward.

Thus Solomon concludes, "There is nothing better for man than to eat, drink, and to enjoy his work. I have seen that even this is from God's hand. For who can eat and who can enjoy life apart from Him?" (2:24–25).

God gives wisdom, knowledge, and joy to those who are pleasing in his sight. The sinner, ignorant of God's pattern, will conversely inherit the task of gathering and accumulating only to give it to the righteous. This statement acknowledges that all the resources belong to God; thus all will ultimately be returned to him.

He gives the power. He gives the know-how. He gives the opportunity. We therefore fly in the face of reality if we try claiming our success as our own. Our work belongs to him just as much as we do.

Once we grasp the truth that God is owner and that our work is a gift from him for our enjoyment, two things begin to happen.

First, *our perspective and attitude changes*. We begin to see the eternal consequences of getting up on Monday morning. The truth is, our arena of professional labor provides our most productive platform for kingdom advance. We are God's movable possessions, his kingdom agents in our sphere of influence. Thus the way we go about our work becomes a powerful kingdom testimony.

I once heard Howard Hendricks tell the story of a flight attendant who served an obnoxious and demanding passenger with unusual calm and kindness. Howard remained behind after the other passengers had deplaned to compliment this young woman on a job well done. In fact, he asked for her name so he could write the airline to tell them about her exceptional performance.

She kindly replied, "Oh, that's not necessary. I don't work for the airline." He was stunned! "You mean, you put up with this obnoxious man, and you don't even work for the airline?"

Seeing his consternation she explained, "They may pay my salary, but I work for the Lord. I couldn't put up with this guy if it were just a job." Truly, when you look at it that way, your profession gives you a daily platform for kingdom advance.

Second, when we understand that our labor is from the hand of the Lord, *we will seek to work in harmony with biblical principles.* By doing so, we will see greater productivity and experience greater enjoyment from our labor.

Don't forget that your labor has eternal significance. As Solomon said to himself, "God will judge the righteous and the wicked, since there is a time for every activity and every work" (Eccl. 3:17).

Kingdom Principles at Work

So let's look at six biblical principles that can help us devote ourselves more fully to him by devoting ourselves to productive labor.

1. *Focus on service.* No one ever exhibited a greater servant spirit than the King, Jesus himself. One of the most disarming events described in the Gospels occurred on the night when Jesus ate the final Passover with his disciples (John 13:1–16). The borrowed room was prepared with everything necessary for the meal, including the basin and towel for the cleansing of their feet. Yet not one of the disciples was willing to engage in this menial task. To their surprise, and perhaps offense, Jesus was the one who kneeled down and washed their feet, telling them that he was giving them an example of service, reminding them that a servant is not greater than his master.

The idea of servanthood is not all that popular in our day. The "service station" has now become a "self-service station." Clerks at convenience stores often give you the impression that you have greatly inconvenienced them.

But if you want to find meaning in your work, look for opportunities to serve. Jesus contrasted those who want to dominate and exercise power over others with those who look first to serve, for these alone have discovered true greatness in the kingdom. "On the contrary, whoever wants to become great among you must be your servant" (Matt. 20:26).

2. *Serve with excellence.* Solomon advised, "Whatever your hands find to do, do with all your strength" (Eccl. 9:10). It is a reproach to our King when we do less than our best and use our spirituality as an excuse.

I once built a relationship with a Jewish business consultant who attended a prayer breakfast I taught. He told me that he used the Shepherd's Guide Business Index—a phone directory of Christian establishments—to know which ones to avoid because many Christian businessmen he had met did poor work. What an indictment! Our philosophy is often, "Do the least you can for the most you can make."

Jesus, on the other hand, taught his followers to go the extra mile (Matt. 5:41). Always exceed expectations. Give good measure in every situation. Every worker's concern ought to be to provide the best product and to give a full day's work for a day's pay. Management ought to provide the best working environment possible and provide good wages and benefits.

James wrote, "Look! The pay that you withheld from the workers who reaped your fields cries out, and the outcry of the harvesters has reached the ears of the Lord of Hosts" (5:4). When laborers and management both strive for excellence, costs will be lower, productivity higher, and satisfied customers will tell others. Think the King is not interested in our daily work? Paul encouraged believers to work "wholeheartedly, fearing the Lord" (Col. 3:22b).

3. *Serve with diligence and enthusiasm.* I can't state this principle nearly as eloquently as Solomon did in the book of Proverbs. "Idle hands make one poor, but diligent hands bring riches" (10:4). "The plans of the diligent certainly lead to profit, but anyone who is reckless only becomes poor" (21:5).

Laziness is not a characteristic of the King, and thus it should not be found among his followers. Paul went beyond sheer diligence with his command about enthusiasm. "Whatever you do, do it enthusiastically, as something done for the Lord and not for men" (Col. 3:23).

4. *Serve with integrity.* If any people ought to be known for their integrity, it should be followers of the King. The writer of Proverbs spoke frequently about integrity in relationship to money and work. "Wealth obtained by fraud will dwindle, but whoever earns it through labor will multiply it" (13:11). "Better a poor man who walks in integrity than someone who has

deceitful lips and is a fool" (19:1). "Making a fortune through a lying tongue is a vanishing mist, a pursuit of death" (21:6).

In one of Jesus' many parables about stewardship (Luke 12:43–46), the key issue was one of trust. The faithful steward was the one who could be trusted.

I often hear people complain about the lack of integrity today. No one seems to be committed to keeping their word, they say. We hear an abundance of excuses, even in the church. But if you commit to do something, follow through. If you are in business, tell the truth about your product.

5. *Work with others.* Solomon discovered the futility of attempting to go it alone. He spoke of seeing someone without any companion, still working to accumulate riches but with no contentment in his wealth (Eccl. 4:8). Solomon's conclusion: "Two are better than one because they have a good reward for their efforts. For if either falls, his companion can lift him up; but pity the one who falls without another to lift him up" (4:9–10). A cord of three strands, he told us, is hard to break.

Jesus' final prayer for his disciples included his desire for their unity in order that they could reflect the unity of the Godhead (John 17:21). Major businesses have discovered that corporate unity is a key to business success.

6. *Be willing to grow.* The book of Ecclesiastes unveils Solomon's willingness to learn. Lest we miss this crucial point, he wrote, "Better is a poor but wise youth than an old but foolish king who no longer pays attention to warnings" (4:13). We are teetering on the brink of disaster when we neglect our need to grow and learn. This book you're reading right now is written with the passion that we will all be willing to learn from the one who wrote the book on life.

Kingdom Purposes at Work

We have talked about *principles* for labor, but we must also consider the *purpose* of labor. If the basic need to earn a living is insufficient to give work meaning, then what is the biblical purpose? Perhaps we will be helped in this quest by first putting aside several *inadequate* purposes for work.

1. *Competition.* We hate to admit that we sometimes work overtime because our motive is to keep up with the "Joneses," whoever they are. Our neighbors buy a new car, and suddenly ours seems so inadequate. You might have guessed, Solomon addressed this matter as well: "I saw that all labor and all skillful work is due to a man's jealousy of his friend. This too is futile and a pursuit of the wind" (Eccl. 4:4). Competition is poor motivation because you are playing a game that you can never win.

2. *Hoarding.* "There is a sickening tragedy I have seen under the sun: wealth kept by its owner to his harm" (Eccl. 5:13). There's a difference between "saving" and "hoarding." We will look later at biblical principles for saving and investing. But the danger of hoarding is that hoarded wealth can remove our trust in God. The one who keeps it locked away never has enough.

3. *Accumulation for inheritance.* In a later section we will look at providing for your children's future. But at this point we should note that a financial inheritance given without biblical management principles can be detrimental to a child's own spiritual financial maturation. We have already noted Ecclesiastes 2:18–23, where Solomon worried about leaving money to a fool who hadn't labored for it.

4. *Pleasure of money itself.* "The one who loves money is never satisfied with money, and whoever loves wealth is never satisfied with income. This too is futile. When good things increase, the ones who consume them multiply; what, then, is the profit to the owner, except to gaze at them with his eyes?" (Eccl. 5:10–11). This verse always reminds me of the entourage of "friends" that flock around the wealthy athlete, consuming what someone else has earned. We earlier noted that God gives us material things to meet our needs and provide pleasure. But when we seek pleasure as an end in itself, it becomes an elusive phantom.

Let's turn our attention now to *positive* purposes that will give meaning to our labor.

1. *To fulfill God's purpose.* "I have seen the task that God has given people to keep them occupied. He has made everything appropriate in its time. He has also put eternity in their hearts" (Eccl. 3:10–11a). In that same context Solomon declared that eating, drinking, and enjoying our labor is a gift of God.

In Luke 16:1–8, Jesus used an example of a corrupt but resourceful steward to teach a lesson about the kingdom potential of money. The steward was confronted with the results of his crooked business transactions. Knowing he would be terminated, he began to make deals with businessmen who owed money to his master, and the servant's master praised him for acting astutely by making friends with his money.

Jesus was not endorsing dishonesty. But he *was* illustrating the truth that sometimes the sons of this age are more astute than sons of the light (v. 8). Sons of light—kingdom-focused Christians—should know that all money belongs to God, and therefore we earn it and use it with eternity in view. Our labor allows us to have the resources to advance God's kingdom. It gives us capital to use for eternal purposes.

2. *To provide a platform for kingdom witness.* In Ephesians 6:5–9, Paul spoke of the need to obey human masters with sincerity of heart. Believers are not to work just to please men but as slaves of Christ. He also spoke to those who are masters over another. *They* must recognize that there is no favoritism with God. So whether we are employee or employer, we must serve as one who knows that the kingdom citizen is called to be salt and light in the marketplace.

3. *To provide for your family.* God allows us to labor with the view of meeting daily needs and living in a productive fashion (Titus 3:14). Paul told young Timothy that the man who doesn't labor to support his own has denied the faith (1 Tim. 5:8).

4. *To share with those less fortunate.* In his farewell address to the Ephesian elders, Paul gave eloquent testimony to this purpose of labor. "You yourselves know that these hands have provided for my needs, and for those who were with me. In every way I've shown you that by laboring like this, it is necessary to help the weak and to keep in mind the words of the Lord Jesus, for He said, 'It is more blessed to give than to receive'" (Acts 20:34–35).

Does your understanding of labor more closely resemble God's viewpoint or that of the world? Are there any areas where you need to bring your thinking into conformity with the directions of the King?

How to Spend Money

"Why do you spend money on what is not food,
and your wages on what does not satisfy."

ISAIAH 55:2A

I know some of you may be thinking: "I certainly don't need a chapter on spending. I can do that quite well by myself."

Well, that's the heart of the problem, isn't it? We buy things we don't need with money we don't have because of advertising we don't believe to impress people we don't really know! Then we resell it in a yard sale.

We are on a spending spree. Americans presently spend $1.20 for every $1.00 they earn.[1] And everybody wants to help us do it. In 2001 banks issued five billion pieces of mail to convince us we need another credit card. This is made even more frightening when we take into account that Americans already have 600 billion dollars of credit card debt. That equals $8,300 per household. And over 50 percent of households nationwide reported difficulty in making the minimum payment required each month. Forty percent of Americans spent more than they earn.[2]

So if we don't learn to manage our spending, we will never be able to save or to give. Thus, if we ignore the Creator's directives in this area of financial management, we will never get out of the debt trap, and we will continue to rob from God, which in turn robs us from experiencing his full blessing.

The Parable of Adequate Preparation

Matthew groups several parables together on kingdom stewardship. These parables follow the section in Matthew's Gospel that speaks about the return of the King (Matt. 24). Therefore, this series of parables makes abundantly clear that stewards will be held accountable for their stewardship.

The first parable (25:45–51) depicts the faithful and sensible steward who has been put in charge of all his master's possessions. Jesus declared that this kind of manager would be found working when the master returns. He then depicted a wicked steward who began to live a life of dissipation because of the delay of the master's return. Jesus warned that the master would return when the servant least expected it, and the servant would be assigned a place with the hypocrites.

While we are most familiar with the third stewardship parable, the parable of the talents (25:14–30), I don't want us to overlook the parable of the ten virgins (25:1–13). The opening word "then" clearly links this parable with the preceding parable of warning. The statement "the kingdom of heaven will be like" does not mean this is a picture of the kingdom, but it is a declaration of what will happen when God's sovereign kingdom purpose reaches its climax with the return of the King.

The maidens can be interpreted either as attendants of the bride or as servants in the bridegroom's home. Normally the bridegroom, along with his close friends, left his home to go to the home of the bride. There were then various ceremonies at the bride's home, followed by a procession through the streets after nightfall as the groom brought his bride home for the wedding feast. The maidens were to assist the bride by meeting the groom as he came from the bride's home. Everyone carried her own lamp, and those persons without a lamp were considered to be party crashers.

In this parable there are five foolish virgins who brought their lamps but did not bring an extra supply of oil in case the groom was delayed. Thus the lamps of the foolish are seen as "going out" (v. 8). These foolish virgins ask the sensible ones to share their oil, but they refuse to do so because there would not be sufficient oil to supply everyone's needs. The foolish bridesmaids are therefore refused entry after the door is shut to the wedding banquet.

The simple but significant truth of the story is that good stewards exercise foresight and planning. It is also important to note that preparedness cannot be shared or transferred. Each of us bears responsibility for our own stewardship.

So the refusal to admit the virgins is not a calloused rejection on the part of the doorkeeper. Far from it! Their failure to plan demonstrated their lack of concern for the kingdom of God, whereas the wise maidens had a plan and prepared for the unexpected.

Have a Plan

If we are going to spend so that we maintain sufficient resources to meet all of our needs, even when the unexpected occurs, we must be like the wise maidens who planned ahead.

The writer of the Proverbs declared: "A plan in the heart of a man is like deep water, but a man of understanding draws it out" (20:5 NASB). "A house is built by wisdom, and it is established by understanding" (24:3). In both cases, the writer of the Proverbs indicated that wisdom dictates thorough planning.

Jesus taught a similar truth to his would-be followers by using an illustration of the man who builds a tower without first calculating the cost (Luke 14:23–29). Do you have a financial plan for your spending? If not, here are five steps for establishing such a plan.

1. *Establish written goals.* As you are writing these goals, saturate the activity with prayer because "a man's heart plans his way, but the LORD determines his steps" (Prov. 16:9).

Begin with simple goal statements. For example, you might begin with a statement such as, "Provide adequately for my family," or, "Increase my level of giving to kingdom enterprises." Next you'll need to establish short-range goals to help you meet these objectives. These may be very short and specific. Pay cash for a new vacuum cleaner. Reduce debt and eliminate it altogether in three years. Start a savings account for my children's college education. Increase giving to kingdom ministries.

2. *Find out where you are at present.* It is a simple but profound truth that you will never get where you want to go until you first know where you are. You must be able to determine your present spending habits. Here are three ideas that may help you:

First, *keep at least two months of detailed records of your regular spending.* Try to anticipate insurance, taxes, and other expenses that may not occur monthly. Second, *do a personal balance sheet.* This doesn't have to be complex. Simply start by adding up your personal assets, including items such as savings accounts, stocks and bonds, retirement accounts, houses, and property. Then list your liabilities—all your outstanding debts. And finally, *estimate your income from all sources.* When you're able to put together these three documents, you will be ready to plan with wisdom.

3. *Establish a budget plan.* A budget is a written program to help you manage God's resources that he has placed at your disposal. Most of the money problems we experience are not the result of insufficient income; they are the result of overspending.

You will be helped in establishing this budget by looking at the spending records you've been keeping. I recommend that you keep your first budget rather simple and somewhat flexible, or it will quickly become your master and not your servant.

Start with large categories such as "tithe, food, housing, clothing." You will then need to break some of these down into smaller categories such as "house payments, utilities, insurance." Larry Burkett suggests that you look at five major divisions—the tithe, taxes, family needs, paying off debts, and developing surplus to respond to others.[3] You could add to this "investing or saving" to build assets with kingdom focus.

4. *Act your wage!* Declare a moratorium on buying consumables with interest spending. Interest is a powerful tool for saving, but it is an equally powerful tool when it works against you. Let's consider a simple example to help us get a clear picture of the trap of overspending.

If a family overspends an average of just $3.35 a day and finances this overage with a credit card (which charges 18 percent annual interest), after ten years this habit of overspending will create a whopping debt of $33,129, with ongoing interest charges of $331 a month. So pray this prayer taken from a paraphrase of Hebrews 13:5: "Lord, help me to be content with what I have and keep my life free from an obsession to spend money on things."

5. *Set a goal for cash purchasing.* As your budget enables you to get a grip on your spending, you will be able to start saving money toward specific goals that will allow you to purchase large items with cash.

Let's take an example of a new car. Suppose you know that you will need different transportation in three years. First, estimate what will be required to purchase the car that best meets your needs. Then calculate what you can expect from the car you'll be trading. Take that amount and divide it into thirty-six monthly payments, and make those payments *to yourself* in an interest-bearing savings account. This will allow you to pay interest to yourself and not the bank.

Practical Tips on Controlling Spending

Finally, just some practical things:

1. *Honestly pray about your purchases.*

2. *Learn to discern the difference between needs, wants, and desires.* "Can I afford it?" and "Do I need it?" are pertinent questions to ask before every purchase.

3. *Ask yourself several questions when considering a purchase not in your budget.* "Will it put a strain on my budget? Will it cause me to neglect giving to the ministry needs through my church? Will it make it difficult for me to meet my long-term savings goals? Will it have a negative impact on my witness?"

4. *Realize that our culture is geared to make us spend.* The advertising industry is aimed at making us discontent with who we are and what we have. We are portrayed as marred, scarred, stretched, and aged. But the cure to all our needs cannot be found in the hot new product. Don't listen to the adversary.

5. *Avoid impulse buying.* Stores are designed to force items on you that you never intended to buy. If you have any hesitancy about purchasing an item, wait.

6. *Avoid shopping when you are depressed.* Many people buy to make themselves feel better. But inevitably the debt incurred only deepens the depression.

7. *Ask the Holy Spirit to help you exercise the fruit of patience and self-control* when it comes to making purchases.

8. *As soon as you purchase anything, turn over the ownership to the Lord.*

9. If you struggle with spending issues, *find an accountability partner.*

I suspect some of you are thinking that you needed this chapter a few years ago. But now the damage has been done, and you are continually battling the budget because of accumulated debt. Good news—we're going to look at how to overcome the bondage of debt in the next chapter.

Week 3, Day 4

How to Get Out of Debt

*"The wicked borrows and does not repay, but
the righteous is gracious and giving."*

PSALM 37:21

Some words have such a profound impact on us that they become etched in our memory. We can remember where we were when we first heard them and how they made us feel at the time.

"Houston, we have a problem!" is one of those collections of words that may elicit such a reaction in you. (It certainly does in me.) When the *Apollo 13* mission to the moon encountered a serious problem, it seemed nearly impossible that the crew would make it back home safely.

But I would say to our nation today, "America, we have a problem!"

In June 2002 the Federal Reserve reported that the total amount of consumer debt was $1.685 trillion. Six hundred billion of that was credit card debt. The repayment of this debt consumes 14 percent of the average family's budget. This means that we have less money to spend on our needs, little to help the poor, and virtually none left for advancing the kingdom.

Many persons end up paying the minimum each month, thus compounding the problem. For example, if you make the minimum payment on the typical credit card balance of $4,800 (assuming a 17 percent interest rate), you can expect to pay on this amount for forty years! You will pay close to $11,000 in interest alone! And this assumes you will charge nothing new during that time.[4] The end result—more than 1.4 million Americans declare personal bankruptcy every year.[5]

Yes, we have a problem!

The movie *Apollo 13* reenacted that incredible drama with heart-pounding intensity. I loved the scene when one of the main NASA officials walked into mission control carrying a box of available parts and challenged the engineers to find a solution. It is easy to define a problem; it's quite another matter to find a solution.

But find a solution we must! Because too much depends on it.

The stability of your family, for example. Some marriage counselors indicate that financial issues are the number one cause of divorce.

Your personal witness is at stake. If you're spending a good deal of time worrying about how to pay for things or biting your nails hoping your paycheck beats your latest bill payments to the bank, your freedom to walk in Spirit-led alertness through the day is going to be seriously threatened.

But beyond that, the advance of the kingdom into every corner of the world is a prime concern that is being ignored because of our "problem." We must solve our debt headache if we are ever going to invade Jerusalem, Judea, Samaria, and the ends of the earth with the gospel if we are going to respond to the heartbeat of God.

Use Credit Wisely

The use of credit and the accompanying debt is an issue where Christian financial planners differ. Some argue that we should avoid credit spending and debt altogether while others recommend discipline and moderation.

We should all at least agree that the Bible warns against *excessive* debt. Proverbs 22:7 bluntly declares, "The rich rule over the poor, and the borrower is a slave to the lender." Further, we should agree that there is wisdom in establishing a plan to pay down our debt, with the goal of ultimately eliminating debt from our budget.

What, then, does the Bible say about debt?

The Israelites had once lived under the Pharaoh's control, and they understood the impact of slavery. Thus Proverbs 22 must have stood as a stern warning to them about the enslaving power of debt. God's desire for Israel was that they would enjoy such abundance that they would do the lending, not the borrowing. "When the LORD our God blesses you as He has promised you, you will lend to many nations but not borrow; you will rule over many nations, but they will not rule over you. If there is a poor person among you, one of your brothers within any of your gates in the land the LORD your God is giving you, you must not be hardhearted or tightfisted toward your poor brother. Instead, you are to open your hand to him and freely loan him enough for whatever need he has" (Deut. 15:6–8).

Think through the obvious implications of this text. The Jews were allowed to loan money to Gentiles at interest. In other passages we find a prohibition against charging "usury" or interest to a fellow Jew (Exod. 22:25; Lev. 25:36; Neh. 5:7) but permission to do so when money was loaned to a Gentile. Still, in every case, excessive usury was condemned. (Notice further that God's concern for the poor echoes throughout this passage.)

Kregg Hood argues that God wants to create a "money-service" culture where financial resources are used as a tool for good and not for selfish greed.[6] The psalmist declared, "Good will come to a man who lends generously and conducts his business fairly" (Ps. 112:5).

Romans 13:8, "Do not owe anyone anything, except to love one another," is used by some financial planners to argue that Christians should not borrow under any conditions. But pay attention to the context. Verses 1–7 are concerned with the state and our relation to it. In that arena, we are definitely to "pay [our] obligations to everyone" (v. 7a)—our taxes, for example. Verse 8, however, brings a transition. We are not simply dealing with taxes and the state at this point but with our obligations to all men. This statement is an imperative, and the gist of it is that we are to have no unpaid debts.

Even if Paul was still referring to financial debts, which some Bible scholars question, this text still does not prohibit borrowing money. "But it does condemn," as John Murray writes, "the looseness with which we contract debts and particularly the indifference so often displayed in the discharging of them."[7]

One final point is worthy of note. If borrowing is categorically prohibited under all circumstances, it would be equally wrong to *profit* from borrowing, which would virtually eliminate the use of every savings investment available to us.

Dr. Hood provides a balanced biblical perspective on debt in his book *Escape the Debt Trap*. In it he comes to three conclusions: (1) it is best not to put yourself in the position of the borrower whenever possible; (2) but borrowing was allowed in Scripture, and interest was not automatically outlawed; so (3) if you must borrow, keep your word about paying it back.[8]

When credit is used to purchase an asset that meets a basic need *and* has the potential to increase in value (such as a house), this is probably a wise use of credit. But when credit is used to finance daily needs, it is unwise and enslaving. At this point we must take scissors to our budget. We are living beyond our means.

The issue of credit spending inevitably brings up the question of using credit cards. Here again, there is room for disagreement. I believe it is acceptable to use credit cards as a tool for effective financial management and to avoid the need to carry large sums of cash. But they should be used for budgeted items and with the agreement of your spouse. You should be able to pay off the entire amount each month. If you can't do so, you are probably overspending.

So get the scissors! If you cannot exercise personal discipline in the use of the credit card, get rid of it.

I guarantee you, the world won't help you here. *Business Today* magazine once ran a story on Walter Caranaugh, a pharmacist with an annual income of $27,000. He had a collection of eight hundred credit cards. And if he had chosen to use them all to their maximum capacity, he would have had a line of credit approaching $9.3 million.

Don't look to the world. Rely on the Holy Spirit to help you control your spending habits.

When Debt Becomes Dangerous

We have already indicated that debt can be incurred under certain conditions with the commitment to repay it in a timely fashion. If this were not allowable, most of us would never own a home except by inheritance. And that home would probably have been bought earlier with debt over a period of time.

But, yes, debt can become dangerous, and it can make us a slave to lending institutions. Debt is dangerous when one of these conditions exists:

1. *When money, goods, or services have been contracted or consumed with payments past due.* In other words, when you can't make monthly payments without credit spending.

2. *When the total of unsecured liabilities exceeds your total assets.* Go back and look at the balance sheet we discussed yesterday.

3. *When the payment on any liability exceeds its asset value.* In other words, if you buy a big-screen TV on credit, the moment you take it out the door, it is worth less than you owe. Remember that.

Buying consumables with credit and incurring the accompanying debt is a sure sign of overspending.

Here are a few guidelines that can be derived from our discussion of dangerous debt.

- Avoid using debt to manage overspending.
- Avoid debt for consumables.
- Use debt wisely for appreciating property such as a home.

Larry Burkett argues that no more than 38 percent of your income should be allocated to housing, including debt retirement.[9]

Failure Is Not Final

Aren't you glad that failure isn't final? I think we love the story of the prodigal son because we can all identify with him. At some point in time or in some arena of life, we have all ignored our Father's Word and have left the security of his home. But like the prodigal, when we came to our senses, we understood the vast goodness our Father had provided. It is God's grace that draws us home.

If you have failed in this matter of financial responsibility, how do you escape the "hog lot" of debt and return to the Father? Here are a few practical steps:

- Admit your failure and ask for forgiveness.
- Determine why you're in debt and how much you owe.
- Commit to a written and balanced budget.
- After your tithe, repay your debt first.
- Sacrifice. It's worth it in the end.
- Apply all additional income to pay down debt.
- Don't accumulate any new debt.
- Learn contentment and practice good money management.
- Never rob God to pay off debts.

Just advance slowly but surely. You didn't get in debt overnight, and you won't solve your problem overnight. Declaring personal bankruptcy is clearly a legal solution, but it is not a spiritual one (Prov. 37:21). Get professional help from a debt counselor if necessary.

And might I be so bold as to suggest that believers should apply these same principles in eliminating their indebtedness to God, in making up for his rightful tithes and offerings that we have spent on ourselves? Can you imagine what resources would be freed up for kingdom advance if believers committed to repay this? Is it possible that our failure in this area may be the reason we struggle so much in other areas of finance?

God challenges us to put him to the test and see if he will not open the windows and pour out blessing (Mal. 3:10).

I pray that we will.

How to Save and Invest

Go to the ant, you slacker! Observe its ways and become wise.

PROVERBS 6:6

Solomon draws our attention to a tiny animal that demonstrates great wisdom—the ant. Without the help of a leader or administrator, this tiny insect prepares provisions in the summer and gathers food during the harvest, laboring with diligence and saving for future need.

He contrasts the ant with those who stay late in bed and fold their arms, too lazy and foolish to concern themselves with thinking ahead. What happens to those who fail to labor and save for the future? "Your poverty will come like a robber, your need, like a bandit" (Prov. 6:11).

How do we measure up to the ant? Americans now save at the lowest rate since the Great Depression—0.5 percent or $5.00 for every $1000 earned.[10] According to the Social Security Administration, diligent saving is the exception and not the rule. The average sixty-five-year-old man today has accumulated less than $100 in free and clear assets.[11]

Maybe it's time we learned something from the ant!

Looking For Balance

As we approach the topic of "saving and investing," we must ask and answer the question, "Why would God have us accumulate wealth if all the resources belong to him?"

Does saving money indicate a lack of faith? After all, we are taught to ask for "daily bread." Further, we remember the rebuke given to the man with a bumper crop whose only solution was to build bigger barns.

On the other hand, we have the illustration of the ant and the positive action of Joseph, who led the Egyptian pharaoh to store crops during the seven years of plenty to provide sufficient resources for the coming famine. Proverbs 21:5 reminds us, "The plans of the diligent certainly lead to profit, but anyone who is reckless only becomes poor."

The key issue seems to be "why" we save. If you read the story of the man with the small barn closely (Luke 12:16–21), you will discover that Jesus didn't reproach him for his productiveness or his plan for saving. The problem was his motive. His aim was "self-centered" rather than "kingdom centered." He used the words *I* and *my* rather than recognizing God's ownership. His reason for accumulating was focused on material pleasure and not on spiritual fulfillment, which was illustrated by his lack of concern for the poor.

Saving and investing are biblical principles, but they must be employed with biblical priorities. Saving can become hoarding if accumulating money becomes the object of our devotion. This attitude often leads to greed and stinginess. It can separate families, spoil children, and breed dishonesty.

On the other hand, saving and investing can also provide for our future needs, both those of our children and grandchildren, while making extraordinary resources available for kingdom advance.

I know we all would like to see that.

Therefore, we should thrill to Paul's words and share his confidence: "God is able to make every grace overflow to you, so that in every way, always having everything you need, you may excel in every good work" (2 Cor. 9:8).

I have found many Christians who agree that it's gracious to give, but they are suspicious of those who accumulate wealth through prudent investments. Clearly, however, we must manage our finances well if we are to give with generous abandon. In Romans 12:8, Paul listed generous giving as an area of spiritual giftedness. Since Paul would have anticipated the tithe as a basic minimum, he must have been referring to those who are gifted to earn and give generously from the surplus.

And that means saving.

Wrong Reasons for Accumulating

Certainly, the process of saving and investing money can be abused and misappropriated, just like any worthy endeavor. That's why in 1 Timothy 6:6–17, Paul gave us sound advice that helps us look at both right *and* wrong motives for saving and investing. If motive is the key issue we must address, let's look first at the ones that are improper and unbiblical.

1. *Envy of others.* The psalmist spoke out powerfully against an envious spirit. And he knew what he was talking about from firsthand, inside experience. "For I envied the arrogant; I saw the prosperity of the wicked" (73:3). In 1 Timothy 6:9, Paul spoke of a downward spiral that can be caused by envy. This temptation is like a lure that creates foolish and harmful desires, which when acted upon, will plunge one into ruin and destruction. When our motive for investing is "keeping up with" or "getting ahead of" the Joneses, it is neither biblical nor satisfying.

2. *Being enamored with the game of making money.* First Timothy 6:9 uses the phrase, "those who want to be rich." When a person becomes charmed by the process of making money, it can quickly become an issue of pride. Money itself becomes secondary at that point. Instead, the thrill of the chase becomes the driving motivator until everybody, including family and friends, becomes a mere pawn in the money-making process. Relationships are sometimes nurtured based on "what someone can do for me."

3. *Building self-esteem.* In 1 Timothy 6:17, Paul told Timothy to warn those who are rich in the present age "not to be arrogant." This is a particularly dangerous motive since money begins to define people whose self-esteem is measured by wealth. They often purchase items that can add to their reputation. They may give generously, but even then they do it with the goal of promoting themselves. We marvel when an overpaid athlete seeks additional millions in salary not because they need it but because another "less gifted" athlete has signed for more money. The writer of Proverbs gave us a strong warning: "Pride comes before destruction, and an arrogant spirit before a fall" (16:18).

4. *The love of money.* People who love money will not part with it, even to build self-esteem. Solomon graphically described the tragedy facing those who approach their finances in this way. "The one who loves money is never satisfied with money, and whoever loves wealth is never satisfied with income. This too is futile" (Eccl. 5:10). Paul simply but profoundly declared that the love of money is the root of all sorts of evil (1 Tim. 6:10), noting that some who crave it will wander away from the faith and pierce themselves with many pains. The man of God is commanded to flee from these things

and pursue righteousness, godliness, faith, love, endurance, and gentleness (6:11).

5. *Accumulation for protection.* This may be the most common error of all, and though it seems reasonable and clearheaded, it goes against kingdom thinking. Many people think they can assure themselves protection though wealth, but God alone is the source of life, happiness, and contentment.

When I moved to Norfolk, I sold a house in Galax, Virginia. I held a second note on it for a few years and then received a lump sum payment. With this sizable sum in hand (to me, anyway), I made an appointment with a friend who worked for a national brokerage firm to get his advice on what I should do with it.

During the interview he asked me what I wanted to accomplish with my savings. I quickly replied, "I want to earn enough to be secure." But his answer to me is one I've never forgotten: "Pastor," he said, "there is no security in money. Only in the Lord."

Great lesson! I should have known that! When we start to assume that our future is secured by money, our accumulated wealth can remove our need to trust in the Lord for what we need. Hear me now—there is nothing wrong with planning and saving God's way, but the person who hoards for protection often loses his conviction that God can supply.

Biblical Reasons for Saving and Investing

If you haven't read 1 Timothy 6:6–19 in its entirety yet, now would be a good time to stop and do so. See if you can find good reasons for saving and investing, like these:

1. *To develop godliness and contentment.* Paul began this entire section with a call to contentment. *Contentment* can be defined as the "invasion of our everyday life with the awareness of God's presence, provision, and protection." Paul puts this into perspective with a stark reminder: "For we brought nothing into the world, and we can take nothing out" (v. 7). Remember, material things are irrelevant at both our entrance and exit from this present world. It is God alone who provides us with material resources for our physical needs (v. 8). In Philippians 4, Paul also gave personal testimony concerning his own contentment. "For I have learned to be content in whatever circumstances I am. I know both how to have a little, and I know how to have a lot" (vv. 11b–12a).

2. *To remind us of God's grace as our ultimate provider.* Look again at 1 Timothy 6:17, where Paul reminds those rich in the present age to set their hope on God "who richly provides us with all things to enjoy." Perhaps

I need to pause a moment to define *rich*. When we look against the backdrop of a global perspective, most hourly employees in America would be considered rich. But the tragedy is that many people attain a level of wealth that enables them to live in relative comfort and forget that God is the provider of all they have.

Certainly, when wealth is kept in proper focus, we can truly enjoy it. My wife's father provides a good case study. He was a hardworking engineer who was taught by his father to give 10 percent and save 10 percent out of each paycheck. God blessed his stewardship, enabling him to help Paula and me attend graduate school in Cambridge. Further, his wealth brought him to a humble and total dependence on God. This led to a joyous desire to give to others in need.

3. *To create a surplus for sharing.* Listen to this principle in Paul's own words: "Instruct them to do good, to be rich in good works, to be generous, willing to share, storing up for themselves a good foundation for the age to come, so that they may take hold of life that is real" (vv. 18–19). This is actually the focal point of the passage. God desires to provide a surplus so that we can be generous and use his resources in such a way that they have impact on the age to come (cp. 2 Cor. 8:14; 9:10–11). While material goods have no eternal significance, they can be shared in such a way that they make an eternal impact. And that's where this whole thing gets really exciting. Ask those who've done it and know from experience!

Generous giving—out of our surplus—enables us to go beyond the foundational level of "tithes and offerings." It frees us from the danger of riches and the tyranny of things (Matt. 19:23–24) and prepares us to experience further blessing. I love the last phrase of this passage—"so that they may take hold of life that is real" (1 Tim. 6:19). Nothing artificial or contrived! Not the fading pleasure that things provide but God's fullness.

Isn't that what we all want?

Practical Suggestions

Here are a few suggestions and goals that might get you started:

1. *Let money work for you.* Avoid "get-rich-quick" schemes. Proverbs 12:11 warns against the one who chases fantasies. Proverbs 21:5 advises a policy of "slow but sure." Save a regular amount each week and increase that amount as you are able. If you save $10 a week for forty years and earn 8 percent on your savings, you would receive $151,265 on an investment of $20,800. If you have trouble saving money, have it deducted from your checking account weekly or monthly. You may find this a painless way to save.

2. *Save with specific goals in mind.* This will keep you focused. For example, you may need to have a savings account for a future purchase of a car, college tuition, or wedding expenses.

3. *Save for short-term emergencies.* Your first goal should be to save money to provide a cash reserve for the unexpected. Many financial planners recommend that you have an amount equal to six months salary available in a readily accessible account.

4. *Invest to create a surplus for sharing.* As you follow biblical principles, you will soon have excess beyond your current needs and a surplus for short-term emergencies. Now you can begin investing. A simple strategy is to use several diversified mutual funds and practice dollar cost averaging. This means that you put a certain dollar amount into these chosen investments each month and ignore the irregularities of the market. If you don't feel competent in the area of investing, you can find books and magazines that will help. Or you may find it necessary to seek professional help for an investment advisor.

Let me give a word of caution, though. Don't forget to tithe the income off your investments and to look for opportunities to give generously. Some people want to wait till they have a large amount before they give any away. We need to use surplus to provide for present ministry needs today before we can be trusted with additional resources for sharing. Giving an appreciated investment is a wonderful way to avoid capital gains and provide for ministry.

5. *Invest for retirement.* It is appropriate to invest money for an adequate retirement, but here again, recognize our human tendency to become hoarders and not investors. Lifestyle changes little after retirement. If anything, the cost of living adjusted for inflation will often be less. Make sure your retirement ideas are compatible with God's. If God blesses you with sufficient resources to retire comfortably, perhaps he is also calling you to a new level of ministry. Volunteer to help at your church or look for mission opportunities. Can you imagine the global impact possible if we would look at our retirement as God's provision for a new mission career?

6. *Invest for your children and grandchildren.* "A good man leaves an inheritance to his grandchildren, but the sinner's wealth is stored up for the righteous" (Prov. 13:22). The amount of the inheritance will vary from family to family. As parents leave money or possessions to their children and grandchildren, they should take into account issues such as management ability and attitudes toward money. Many believers do not consider the consequences of leaving large amounts of money in the hands of irresponsible children. Solomon despaired over leaving his wealth to a foolish son

(Eccl. 2:19). Your goal as a parent is not to make your children wealthy but to shape them into the image of Christ. Some parents may want to give occasional gifts of money during their own lifetime. If so, this gift should not be given with strings attached but with biblical instruction for management. Explain how you came by the excess that enabled you to provide this gift.

Paula and I recently enjoyed giving our adult children a cash gift as the result of an inheritance we had received. When I gave my children the checks, I also gave them a note indicating the money management principles by which I have conducted my life. This gift helped my children meet present needs, but it also provided an opportunity to teach biblical principles of money management.

When considering how much to leave your children, here are a few questions that might help: (1) Have I caused my children to covet money? (2) Will this amount help them learn better management principles? (3) Have they displayed attitudes and management abilities that would enable them to manage this amount of money without being wasteful? (4) Am I providing for them or offering protection? (5) Will this gift help them learn to give from their newfound abundance?

When we speak of saving for inheritance, it also assumes that the Christian steward will have a will in place to ensure that the surplus God has provided is used according to our desires. Having an up-to-date will is an issue of stewardship.

Paula and I have had wills in place for most of our married life, largely designed—especially in our younger years—to care for our three daughters in the event of our death. Last year, however, we updated our wills because we decided to adopt a fourth "child" that will receive an equal share of our estate. That fourth child is made up of several ministries that we believe will help to reach the nations.

We had a family conference explaining our plan and our passion to our now-grown children. They were thrilled to know we would be practicing the same level of stewardship in death that we have in life. By funding these charities first out of our estate and annuities, our children will each receive about the same amount they would otherwise.

You may want to consider something like this yourself.

Don't forget that one of the reasons God provides excess resources is because his heartbeat is that all the nations come to know him as their King. All of our reasons for saving and investing should nestle inside this overarching challenge and truth.

Still Giving after All These Years

Week 4, Day 1

The King Wants You

Therefore, brothers, by the mercies of God, I urge you to present your bodies as a living sacrifice, holy and pleasing to God; this is your spiritual worship.

ROMANS 12:1

Many of my boyhood memories have faded. But for some reason I can still remember that military recruiting poster that declared, "Uncle Sam Wants You." Those were days of national pride when many volunteered for service out of a sense of love for the country and appreciation for the freedoms we enjoy.

There is a higher calling, however, that comes from the sovereign King of the universe—"I want you!" It is a call that emerges out of the incredible truth that God has redeemed us from our sin through his great mercy. It is a call that affirms the fact that we possess something to offer to God that has already been declared to be both "holy" and "pleasing." Too many Christians labor under the mistaken impression that they have little to offer to God. They are content to serve God in their "poor, weak way."

Hold your head up! You are a child of the King. And he wants you!

In the course of this chapter, I'd like us to break apart the first two verses of Romans 12, letting them show us what God really wants from us. It's probably more than you think, but so is the reward of giving him everything.

The Basis of the Demand

The requirement that we "present our bodies as living sacrifice" might seem extreme if it were not placed in the context of the "mercies of God." You may have noticed that verse 1 begins with "therefore." It links this directive with all that had gone before in Paul's letter to the church in Rome, particularly chapters 9 through 11. The "mercies of God" is a good summary statement for the early part of this epistle.

Paul had already referred to the mercy of God nine times prior to this verse—Romans 9:15 (twice), 16, 18, 23; 11:30, 31 (twice), 32. Truly, his mercy is everywhere in the gospel message and can never be separated from his love, his grace, and his faithfulness. God's mercy, as taught throughout the Old Testament, was made clear in the atoning work of Christ (Heb. 2:17).

In chapters 9–11, Paul demonstrated how God had made it possible for Jew and Gentile alike to be saved based on his mercy, not human effort. The only person who could save a human race that was lost in sin was a merciful God, who "imprisoned all in disobedience, so that He may have mercy on all" (Rom. 11:32). At this point Paul broke into praise about the riches of the wisdom and knowledge of God. Mercy prompted God to take on himself the penalty we deserved, full punishment for our sin, to give us what we could never earn—forgiveness and eternal life.

Know this: doctrine is never taught in Scripture simply to be known, but so that it may be translated into action. It is much more verb than noun. That's why Jesus told his disciples, "If you know these things, you are blessed if you do them" (John 13:17). Nothing less than obedience and radical abandon can be an adequate response to the mercies of God.

The Extent of the Sacrifice

All the language of this verse echoes that of the Old Testament sacrificial system. Words like *sacrifice, present, holy,* and *pleasing* are virtually technical terms of sacrifice. What does God desire, and what does God deserve? Nothing more and nothing less than our whole selves!

Body here means the whole human person, including all the means of expressing oneself. We are greatly mistaken if we think God wants or needs our tithe to accomplish his work. That misconception grows out of an overestimation of our worth and an underestimation of God's resources. *God wants us,* not our money! And he deserves and will accept nothing less.

Authentic worship will always be accompanied by sacrifice. In the Old Testament man brought an animal sacrifice to God. But under the New Covenant, man becomes the sacrifice that is brought to God. In the Old Testament there were sacrifices for sin as well as sacrifices expressing gratitude and praise. But thanks be to God, Christ has fulfilled once for all the sacrifice for sin (Heb. 9:26; 10:10, 12, 14). And now by his mercy he permits us to present ourselves to him as a sacrifice of praise.

Truly, just being able to present our lives to him is a gift in itself.

In case you missed the point, God is not asking you to dedicate your money, time, talents, influence, creativity, or anything else to him. He only desires you! Because when he has all of you, you will know that you have nothing else to bring.

Oswald Chambers eloquently stated this truth. "We have the idea that we can dedicate our gifts to God. However, you cannot dedicate what is not yours. There is actually only one thing you can dedicate to God, and that is the right to yourself. If you will give God your right to yourself, he will make a holy experiment of you, and his experiments always succeed. The one true mark of a saint of God is the inner creativity that flows from being totally surrendered to Jesus Christ."[1]

Just to be sure we are all clear on the gift God desires, I would remind you that what he wants is the very body he has delivered from death and sin. "For we know that our old self was crucified with Him in order that sin's dominion over the body may be abolished" (Rom. 6:6a). In that same context Paul declared, "And do not offer any parts of it to sin as weapons for unrighteousness. But as those who are alive from the dead, offer yourselves to God, and all the parts of yourselves to God as weapons for righteousness" (6:13).

God is good! He has given us the only gift he desires.

The Value of the Gift

I also love the phrase "holy and pleasing to God." *Holy* simply means that our bodies are to be set apart for his service. *Pleasing* assures us that what we offer has already been approved.

I find this truth to be encouraging. We have something to offer to God that he desires and has already approved.

Further, Paul declared that the giving of our body is our "spiritual worship." The word translated *spiritual* is the Greek word *logikon*. The adjective means "pertaining to the *logos* or reason." Epictetus, a stoic philosopher of the late first century wrote, "If I were a nightingale I would do what is proper to a nightingale . . . but in fact I am a rational (*logikos*) creature, so I must praise God."[2]

Yes, worship is the anticipated and appropriate response of one who has experienced God's mercy. In truth, all men owe both obedience and worship to their Creator, but the one who has a clear perception of God's mercy is the one who sees it as both privilege and obligation.

Worship consists not simply in the singing of hymns, the recitation of Scripture, and the giving of tithes; it is the presentation of one's entire being to God. And once this gift has been offered, you will never again struggle with the gift of time, talents, or money. All of these are merely the outward expression of the offering of *you*.

The Ongoing Transformation

Even those who have experienced the "mercies of God" are susceptible to the lure of this age. "This age" refers to the existing framework of human society still impacted by the power of the adversary.

In Galatians 1:4, Paul called our time in history "this present evil age." It is dominated by Satan, the god of this age who "has blinded the minds of the unbelievers so they cannot see the light of the gospel of the glory of Christ, who is the image of God" (2 Cor. 4:4; cp. 1 Cor. 2:6).

But a new age has dawned for those who are in Christ Jesus and have been raised up in resurrection life with him, enabling them to walk in a new way of life (Rom. 6:3–4). Through the gift of the Spirit, believers have already received the firstfruits of this new existence (Rom. 8:23), which means we are no longer under obligation to the flesh (8:12) and are as free as we want to be from the pull of this age.

It is possible for us, while dwelling temporarily on this earth, to live our lives as heirs of the age to come. In truth, this is what it means to be kingdom minded. In Christ we have become a new creation. "Therefore if anyone is in Christ, there is a new creation; old things have passed away, and look, new things have come" (2 Cor. 5:17).

When believers, who already belong to the age to come, allow the present age to influence their thinking, the result is sheer dissonance. Kingdom citizens cannot live by the wisdom of the world, instead they must surrender themselves to the wisdom of God contained in his Word (cp. 1 Cor. 2:6). Do your decisions about the use of time, gifts, influence, and money clearly reflect the "age to come," or is your thinking on these matters still being influenced by the "present age"?

Another great turn of phrase included in this familiar passage from Romans 12 reveals the total contrast between being "conformed" and being "transformed." We must continually "be transformed by the renewing of our mind." The Greek word translated "transformed" is *metamorphoo*, from which we get the English word *metamorphosis*. This term is used in Matthew 17:2 and Mark 9:2 to describe the transfiguration of Jesus. The only other use in the New Testament is found in 2 Corinthians 3:18, "We all, with unveiled faces, are reflecting the glory of the Lord and are being transformed into the same image from glory to glory; this is from the Lord who is the Spirit." The Holy Spirit brings about this spiritual transformation when we present ourselves as a living sacrifice to the Lord.

But the transformation process is accomplished by the "renewing" of the mind. The word translated "renew" is used in two other contexts that help us understand our present passage. In 2 Corinthians 4:16, Paul wrote, "Therefore we do not give up; even though our outer person is being destroyed, our inner person is being renewed day by day." Rather than focusing on the affliction he was experiencing, he focused instead on the incomparable eternal glory. Then he gave us the key in verse 18: "So we do not focus on what is seen, but on what is unseen; for what is seen is temporary, but what is unseen is eternal."

Most of our spending and giving problems occur when we focus on the seen rather than the unseen. Kingdom people, however, have the vision to see beyond the present age to the age to come because the Spirit is renewing their minds.

In Colossians 3:8–9, Paul instructed believers to put away anger, wrath, malice, slander, filthy language, and lying. These are characteristics of the old man whose life is conformed to this age. Believers, however, have put on a new man, "who is being renewed in knowledge according to the image of his Creator" (3:10). While it is the work of the Spirit to renew our minds, there must be the cooperation of the human will. We must be willing to "put off" and "put on."

Finally, I must say that I love "so that" phrases in Scripture. They affirm that which we have been empowered to do. And Romans 12 gives us a "so that" which encapsulates one of our greatest desires and assures its positive result. We can discern "what is the good, pleasing, and perfect will of God."

This does not simply mean that we can *know* the will of God; it means we can *perform* the will of God.

We discover the will of God through the study of his Word. And as we study his Word, the Holy Spirit illumines our minds and empowers us to obey him, which in turn allows us to overcome the pull of the world and prove the will of God.

One night I was visiting with a layman from First Baptist, Norfolk. We were in the home of a single mom who was living with a man who was not her husband. As we attempted to share the gospel, she continually wanted us to counsel her concerning the struggles she was facing in life. Finally the layman said, "I will stay here all evening and give you all the advice I can if you will first answer three simple questions."

She quickly consented.

He first asked her if she was certain she was a born-again follower of Christ. She responded with an enthusiastic yes.

He then asked her if she believed the Bible was the inerrant Word of God that contained absolute truth about every matter of life. She again gave a positive response.

Finally he asked her if she would be willing to obey anything he could show her from the Bible that would shed light on her life. But when she heard the final question, she began to make excuses based on her unusual circumstances. When she finished with her protestations, he calmly started over with question one.

Are you stuck on that third question, too? Is there anything God has said to you about your time, money, or talents that you are presently disobeying? Are you willing to say yes to God and no to this age?

Don't worry—the Holy Spirit will empower you to do the will of God.

Week 4, Day 2

Giving Through the Ages

He blessed him and said, "Abram is blessed by God Most High, Creator of heaven and earth, and give praise to God Most High who has handed over your enemies to you." And Abram gave him a tenth of everything.

GENESIS 14:19–20

Tithing is as old as history itself.

When Abram left Ur of the Chaldeans on a pilgrimage of faith, he was promised God's blessing in order that he and his descendants would bless the peoples of the earth. Abram and his nephew Lot, you remember—along with their families and numerous belongings—began their journey traveling together until Lot determined to head for Sodom and Gomorrah. But this area was in political turmoil; so Chedorlaomer took Lot and all his possessions captive. Only a brave rescue mission by Abram and the three hundred trained men among his household was able to save Lot, as well as the other citizens of Sodom. Abram had returned a victorious deliverer, having recovered the goods and people of an entire city.

After this successful venture, Abram was met by the king of Salem, who is simply identified in Scripture as a priest of God Most High (El Shaddai). In sheer gratitude Abram offered him a tenth of everything he had.

97

Then the king of Sodom offered Abram all the spoils of war, treasures that Abram might have considered a just reward for his heroic efforts. But Abram refused to take anything from him, lest the king would boast, "I made Abram rich" (Gen. 14:23). In other words, Abram had learned that God is the rightful owner of heaven and earth and that he alone had given Abram victory. The gift of a tithe to Melchizedek was based on the recognition that God was owner and provider.

Abraham's grandson Jacob also had a profound experience with God at Bethel. In a dream God renewed to Jacob the promise that had been given to Abraham (Gen. 28:14). When Jacob awoke, he set up a marker and made a vow with God. "This stone that I have set up as a marker will be God's house, and I will give to You a tenth of all that You give me" (28:22).

Therefore, it is apparent from these repeated instances in Israel's earliest history that the patriarchs practiced tithing before the law was given. It was a simple act of gratitude in recognition of God's provision.

And as we look to the Old Testament for a model of giving, we discover that Israel continued to be given numerous opportunities for worshipping God through tithes and offerings.

Old Testament Offerings

The first worship offering that was prescribed for all of Israel was the offering of the firstborn.

In Exodus 13, immediately after the exodus from Egypt, Moses gave the people instructions in preparation for the taking of the Promised Land. These specific directions dealt with the feast of unleavened bread, which was virtually the same as Passover. Israel was told to *consecrate* every firstborn male from the womb. "To consecrate" means to consider that it belongs to the Lord.

Moses further instructed them that when they took possession of the land of promise, they were to offer the firstborn males of all their livestock as a sacrifice. Those animals considered unclean were to be replaced by another.

The firstborn son, too—though not to be *sacrificed*, of course—was still to be redeemed (Exod. 13:12–13), an idea that seems to mean "to buy back for a price." God declared, "But I redeem all the firstborn of my sons" (v. 15). According to Numbers 3:11–13, God fulfilled the requirement of the redemption of the firstborn sons by choosing the Levites for himself. They would represent the firstborn of all Israel.

But I don't want to get bogged down in the details of this offering and miss the significance of the gift of the firstborn.

In Exodus 13:3, Moses told the Israelites that this practice would remind them that "the Lord brought you out of here by the strength of His hand." He instructed the fathers in verse 8: "On that day explain to your son, 'This is because of what the LORD did for me when I came out of Egypt'" (see also 13:14). They were to remember, from generation to generation, that God had redeemed them from the bondage of Egypt. This offering of the firstborn was both a reminder and a celebration.

We can't avoid looking ahead. Jesus himself was brought to the temple as a baby, based on this law of the firstborn (Luke 2:22–24). The New Testament declares that he is the firstborn of the Father (Heb. 1:6), the first-born of creation (Col. 1:15), and the firstborn from the dead (Rev. 1:5). God redeemed sinful man by the gift of his firstborn so that we could be called the "assembly of the firstborn" (Heb. 12:23).

So it's easy to see that this offering of the firstborn is truly significant, as were the other offerings established in the Old Testament, including those surrounding the three major feasts of the Israelites. Let's look at those.

In Exodus 23:14–19 (see also 34:18–26), Israel was called to "celebrate a festival in My honor three times a year" (v. 14). The first was the Feast of Unleavened Bread, which was a memorial of deliverance.

The second was related to the harvest of the firstfruits. Choice examples of the crop were to be brought to the house of the Lord (v. 19) to be used for the support of the priests (Num. 18). According to Deuteronomy 26:1–11, these offerings were to be brought in a basket for presentation in the sanctuary. The first sheaf of the new crop of barley was presented as a wave offering before the Lord. Can you imagine the pageantry and beauty as Israel waved the sheaves of barley and brought baskets heavy laden with the bounty of the land and placed them on the altar?

The third festival offering, called the Festival of Ingathering or Festival of Booths, occurred at the end of the year, "when you gather your produce from the field" (v. 16). The dwelling in booths (Lev. 23:42; Deut. 16:14) was a joyful reminder of God's presence, provision, and protection.

But there was a word of warning concerning all of these celebrations: "No one is to appear before Me empty-handed" (Exod. 23:15; 34:20). These festivals provided Israel with the opportunity of celebrating in God's presence, reminding them that he had redeemed them and had met their every need.[3]

We also find that on several occasions, the Israelites were given the privilege of participating in freewill offerings. These were related to specific events, such as the construction of the tabernacle or the temple, or the rebuilding of the wall.

The offering related to the tabernacle is particularly illustrative. Moses instructed them, "Take up an offering for the LORD among you. Let everyone whose heart is willing bring this as the LORD's offering" (Exod. 35:5a). They were allowed to bring tangible items such as gold, yarns, linens, ram skins, and gemstones. The skilled craftsmen were called to give their skills as gifts to God. "So the Israelites brought a freewill offering to the LORD, all the men and women whose hearts prompted them to bring something for all the work that the LORD, through Moses, had commanded to be done" (v. 29).

Notice the two emphases: they gave from a *willing heart* and they *gave to the Lord.*

The Offering of the Tithe

The tithe was equivalent to a tenth part of all the produce and livestock that God graciously provided for Israel. "Every tenth of the land's produce, grain from the soil or fruit from the trees, belongs to the LORD; it is holy to the LORD. . . . every tenth animal from the herd or flock, which passes under the shepherd's rod" (Lev. 27:30, 32).

If a farmer or shepherd wanted to keep a portion of the tithe, he could redeem it by adding one-fifth to its value (27:32). The tithe not only celebrated God's provision, but it also reminded them that God was the true owner of the land (Lev. 25:23). If you read the entirety of Leviticus 27, you will find that the directions concerning the tithe are in the context of honoring one's vows. Thus the tithe was considered a *vow,* a promise that one was honor bound not to violate.

Numbers 18:21–32 indicates that the tithe was received by the Levites and was to be used for their support and ministry since they had no inheritance in the land. Deuteronomy 12 and 14 add further to our understanding of the tithe, showing us that on numerous occasions (12:11, 14, 18, 21, 26; 14:24) the people were specifically told where they were to bring their tithes. "Then the LORD your God will choose the place to have His name dwell. Bring there everything I command you; your burnt offerings, sacrifices, offerings of the tenth, personal contributions, and all your choice offerings you vow to the LORD" (12:11).

The place where God's name dwelt would have been the tabernacle or the temple. They were not to take the tithes to a place of their own choosing but to the place designated by the Lord. This is probably what Malachi meant when he declared, "Bring the full 10 percent into the storehouse so that there may be food in My house" (3:10a).

An additional tithe is mentioned in Deuteronomy 14:28–29: "At the end of every three years, bring a tenth of all your produce for that year and store it within your gates. Then the Levite, who has no portion or inheritance among you, the foreign resident, fatherless, and widow within your gates may come, eat, and be satisfied. And the LORD your God will bless you in all the work of your hands that you do." The tithe not only recognized God's provision but also prepared Israel for further blessing.

I find it fascinating that the Deuteronomic code required that the tithe of agriculture be used in a family feast celebrating God's provision and presence. "You are to feast there in the presence of the LORD your God and rejoice with your family" (14:26b). We often view the presentation of tithes and offerings as an issue of strict adherence to the law, but for Israel it was a celebration of abundance in the presence of the Lord. Can you imagine the impact these celebrations of grace must have had on Israel's pagan neighbors?

It can hardly be overstated that the tithe was considered an important aspect of worship. Malachi wrote in a period when conditions in Israel were turbulent and despair was spreading. He pointedly asked and answered a question that he believed to be at the heart of the problem. "'Will a man rob God? Yet you are robbing Me!' You ask: 'How do we rob you?' 'By not making the payments of 10 percent and the contributions'" (Mal. 3:8). The result was that they were suffering under a curse. In other words, they had forfeited God's presence, provision, and protection.

When I was pastor in Norfolk, Virginia, a group of petty thieves began to prey on churches during worship service. They would steal from the cars in the parking lots and loot purses that were left in the choir room while the choir was leading worship. When they hit First Norfolk, the press showed up to do a story on the Sunday morning vandals. During the interview they asked if I was surprised that someone would steal from people while they were at church.

Without really thinking through my reply, I responded that I wasn't at all surprised since many of the people who sat before me in the pews stole from God every Sunday, when they kept back his tithes and offerings.

The reporter and some of our church members were stunned by my response. Perhaps I should have been a bit more diplomatic. Nonetheless, it is hard to believe that someone who claims to be a follower of Christ, who has experienced the grace of God in redemption and daily provision, would ever consider coming into God's presence with empty hands. Why would we forfeit the pleasure of worshipping the King with tithes and offerings?

Clearly, this is the standard and legacy of Old Testament worship. As we shall see in the next chapter, it remains a key ingredient of godly obedience in the New Testament as well.

Week 4, Day 3

Jesus on Tithing

*Woe to you, scribes and Pharisees, hypocrites! You pay a tenth of mint, dill,
and cumin, yet you have neglected the more important matters
of the law—justice, mercy, and faith. These things should have
been done without neglecting the others.*

MATTHEW 23:23

I have always been surprised that people who claim to be followers of Christ attempt to use Scripture, taken out of context, to avoid the obvious implication of the teaching of biblical principles.

Over the years I have encountered people who wanted to argue that tithing was a matter of legalism and thus inappropriate for a person now under grace. But this argument is flawed from the beginning since the first two instances of tithing (Gen. 14; 28) occur before the giving of the law.

Further, one would be hard pressed to find support for the idea that someone who has experienced the amazing grace of our Lord, made available through the cross, would desire to do less than someone under the law. Such a position would be a disgrace to grace!

Others retreat to the argument of silence. They surmise that since tithing is mentioned infrequently by Jesus, it can't be that important. But how many times must something be taught in God's Word before it becomes important to the committed follower of Christ? It is likely that tithing was seldom mentioned by Jesus because he anticipated that these basic matters were clearly understood by all!

But let's look at what the New Testament does say about tithing.

The Bare Minimum

The Pharisees were the largest and most influential religious-political party during New Testament times. They were the legalists of the New Testament era, fancying themselves as the guardian of the law. As the leaders of the synagogue, they had great influence and exercised significant control over the general population, firmly believing that the way to God was through obedience to the law. They had developed an oral tradition to protect the written law, and they often opposed Jesus because he refused to accept the oral law.

The context of Matthew 23:23 is a denunciation of the scribes (experts in the Law) and of the Pharisees. There are seven specific charges, each of them beginning with the phrase, "Woe to you, scribes and Pharisees, hypo-crites!" Following this introduction, there is a brief cameo illustrating their failure to live up to their claim to be the guardians of the law.

The fourth woe in particular relates to their practice of tithing as taught in Old Testament law. As you would expect, these legalists had been so meticulous in their observance of the law that they had tithed everything, even down to their garden herbs. Can you see one of the Pharisees down on his knees counting out his mint, dill, and cumin? Yet Jesus claimed they had neglected weightier issues, such as justice, mercy, and faith. This trio of character qualities recalls the summary of true religion given by the prophet Micah (6:8). Jesus echoed the concern of the Old Testament prophets that inner righteousness is what gives meaning to outward ritual.

Notice, however, that Jesus was not condemning their act of tithing. He made this clear with his statement, "These things should have been done without neglecting the others" (v. 23).

We can't miss the obvious implication. Jesus assumed that they would understand and practice tithing. This they should do! Yet they should have also understood that to practice the detail of the law while ignoring its spiritual value made them like a blind guide who stooped to drink, pushing aside a tiny gnat and carelessly swallowing a camel.

Thus, for someone to use this passage to argue against the principle of tithing puts that person in the same category with the blind guides of Jesus' day. Camels aren't easy to swallow!

In Luke 18:9–14 we find another instance of tithing in Jesus' teaching, the parable of two men who went up to the temple to pray. One was a tax collector who was so overwhelmed by his sin that he couldn't even look up to heaven. The other was a Pharisee, who in his pride thanked God that he was not like other people—not greedy, not unrighteous, not an adulterer—and especially not like this tax collector!

He then cited this proof for his boast: "I fast twice a week; I give a tenth of everything I get" (v. 12). All we can conclude from this text is that tithing was still being practiced in Jesus' day as normative religion.

Jesus and the Law

Further proof. It is likely that more legalistically inclined Jews, such as the scribes and Pharisees, were scandalized by Jesus' radical attitude toward the Sabbath and the laws regarding uncleanness. They feared that this popular rabbi had set out to destroy the law and the prophets. ("The law and the prophets" is a Jewish way of referring to the entire Old Testament.)

But in the Sermon on the Mount, Jesus made a bold declaration about his relationship to the law. "Don't assume that I came to destroy the Law or the Prophets. I did not come to destroy but to fulfill" (Matt. 5:17).

While debate exists among Bible scholars as to the actual meaning of this statement, it seems best to translate it in terms of "bringing to completion." Jesus in his life and teaching provided the "final revelation of God's will to which the Old Testament pointed forward, and which now transcends it."[4] Paul made the same point in Romans 10:4—"For Christ is the end of the law for righteousness to everyone who believes."

So the entirety of the Old Testament—law and prophets—pointed forward to what Jesus brought into being through the incarnation. His ministry, rather than diminishing the law, brought it to full measure by supplying the final revelation of the will of God. Far from abolishing Old Testament revelation, Jesus was its intended culmination. The writer of Hebrews made a similar point. "Long ago God spoke to the fathers by the prophets at different times and in different ways. In these last days, He has spoken to us by His Son" (1:1–2a).

Just a few verses later in his Sermon on the Mount (Matt. 5:18–20), Jesus set a new standard for kingdom citizens that far exceeded the righteousness of the scribes and Pharisees. The kingdom citizen, he said, should go beyond lip service and legalistic observance of the law. Rather, he should internalize the law so that his life and teaching are molded by God's Word.

We might look to Matthew 15:1–20 as an example. The Pharisees and scribes wanted to know why Jesus' disciples broke the tradition of the elders concerning the washing of hands when they ate. But Jesus gave examples of how the legalists had actually broken God's commandments by their adherence to man-made traditions. He quoted Isaiah's statement about people who honor God with the lips but whose heart is far from him. He then explained to the crowd that defilement comes from within, not from without.

In Matthew 5:21–48, Jesus again illustrated this new kingdom ethic built on Christ's fulfillment of the law. There are six units of teaching in this passage, each introduced by the phrases, "You have heard that it was said," and, "But I tell you." This wasn't intended to be a complete statement of Jesus' ethical teaching but rather a series of varied examples that show how the principles of verses 17–20 work in actual practice.

Without attempting to look at each, we can get the pattern from the first. Jesus quoted the prohibition on murder: "You have heard that it was said to our ancestors, 'Do not murder'" (v. 21). But then he went beyond the issue of actual murder, condemning the anger in one's heart as the fire that leads to murder—an anger that is just as worthy of guilt as the act of murder itself. The attitude of the heart is so vital, in fact, that when a worshipper remembers that his brother has something against him, he is to leave his gift at the altar and seek reconciliation (v. 21–24).

In each case Jesus' ethical teaching was more demanding than the law. Kingdom ethics are not thin and external but intensified and internalized. Jesus was looking for obedience that came from the heart, an obedience that truly impacts our motives and attitudes. It is apparent that such intensified standards are impossible for us to obey and thus must be produced by the Holy Spirit who indwells the believer (see the promise of Ezek. 36:27).

Since our specific goal in this section is to understand how Old Testament principles of tithing and offerings were applied in the teaching of Jesus, we should also look at the verses that introduce his teaching on prayer (Matt. 6:1–4); for these, too, give us insight into Christ's perspective on giving.

The central issue of chapter 6 is how one practices righteousness (v. 1). Jesus selected almsgiving, prayer, and fasting as examples of religious observance. This trio represented the three most important requirements for personal piety in mainstream Judaism. Almsgiving was a religious duty and not a personal option.

The first statement—"whenever you give to the poor"—denotes that Jesus expected his followers to give generously. The difference was that they were not to "sound a trumpet before you, as the hypocrites do" (v. 2). In other words, they were not to call attention to their great generosity.

Notice that the issue is not whether a disciple gives. That's just assumed! It is the attitude and the motive that now must conform to the heart of God.

More, Not Less

To interact with verses like these from Jesus' teaching and still conclude that tithes and offerings are artificial requirements, that minimal giving should be acceptable under the circumstances—as though living under grace gives us permission not to take our kingdom responsibilities too seriously—is to give our human nature far too much credit. Grace should free us not to do less but to do more, not to earn God's favor but to let it continue transforming us.

It may be true that some preachers have used less than the best motives for extracting the tithe (such as guilt). But that doesn't alter the biblical teaching. Don't let such an approach steal your joy in giving. Tithing, like prayer, is never to be used as a tool to bribe God. It is not a get rich scheme. Nor should it ever be used as a tool to buy influence or manipulate the direction of the church. The attitude that says, "I'll withhold my tithe until they do such and so" goes to the issue of motive and attitude, which Jesus clearly addressed.

But as we noted in the last chapter, tithing is not the only aspect of giving. We will return in subsequent days to look at other New Testament texts that will help us have a fuller understanding of our stewardship opportunities, helping us see how grace liberates us to go beyond the tithe and give proportionately, generously, and joyously.

Week 4, Day 4

Open the Floodgates

"Bring the full 10 percent into the storehouse so that there may be food in My house. Test Me in this way," says the LORD of Hosts. "See if I will not open the floodgates of heaven and pour out on you a blessing for you without measure."

MALACHI 3:10

The news sounded too good to be true! One of my deacons was calling to tell me that he had a copier he wanted to give to our church. This was good news because we were still using an ancient mimeograph machine, and this man was a leading salesman for a company that produced the finest copiers on the market.

The copier he unloaded on us, however, was huge and dated. It must have been a first-generation model. I know you're not supposed to "look a gift horse in the mouth," but this one had a mouthful of cavities. I asked him if the copier could be repaired if it broke down. He confessed it was dated and that parts probably weren't available.

Finally, I asked him, "Would you use this in your business?" He replied that it wasn't sufficient for his work.

I then asked him why he had given it to the church. His reply stunned me, "Well, I figured it was good enough for the church."

But how could it be good enough for God if it wasn't sufficient for use in a business—an enterprise that would never impact the nations for the kingdom of God?

This event reminds me of the situation in Malachi's day. Malachi, the last of the Old Testament prophets, wrote around four hundred years before Christ during a time of spiritual malaise. Religious practice was in such disarray that God told the people they should shut the door to the temple to prohibit the kindling of useless fire (1:11).

People were bringing blind, lame, and sick animals for their sacrifices (1:8). The family was in disarray, with men divorcing their rightful wives and marrying pagan women (2:11–15), and there was a general neglect of social wrongs (3:5).

Nevertheless, the Lord declared his great love for Israel and offered to bring them restoration and abundance.

Why?

I Have Loved You

The opening affirmation of this book echoes from the heavens— "I have loved you" (Mal. 1:2). This is a Hebrew perfect tense of the verb that signifies that God's love is a completed action. He had previously announced his love for Israel centuries before (Deut. 7:7–8), and that love remained in effect in spite of her present apostasy.

This is hard even for Christians to believe sometimes, not to mention those who haven't yet received the grace of God. But his love proceeds from his character. It is an unconditional covenant love that is never merited by the recipient but flows unabated from the heart of God.

Certainly the greatest demonstration of God's love was the sending of his own Son to become our sin offering (John 3:16). But God's love is of the same level, intensity, and design whether it is expressed in Old Testament images or declared through the incarnation.

In spite of the many demonstrations of his steadfast love, Israel—like an angry, spoiled child—continued to question it, asking, "How have You loved us?" (Mal. 1:2). They had become so insensitive to God's daily blessings that they brashly demanded that God prove his love.

Their questions had been prompted by God's judgment of Edom—the nation that was descended from Jacob's brother Esau—for being "immoral" and "godless" (Gen. 36:1–8; Heb. 12:16). I suppose the Israelites were guilty, like we too often become, of sentimentalizing love to such a degree that we separate it from judgment and punishment. But God cannot truly love without judging the sin that destroys the fabric of his beloved.

God asked them some penetrating questions in response—"A son honors his father, and a servant his master. But if I am a father, where is My honor? And if I am a master, where is your fear of Me? says the LORD of Hosts to you priests, who despise My name" (Mal. 1:6).

The priests and the people both gave lip service concerning their love of God, but their careless, haphazard, and profane service had made another statement. This lack of honor and service is placed in bold relief by the majesty of God—"'For I am a great King,' says the LORD of Hosts, 'and My name will be feared among the nations'" (1:14b). They had treated the King with less honor than a son would show his earthly father.

Israel's Response to Love

But Israel stubbornly questioned God once again—"How have we despised Your name?" (1:6b). God responded, "By presenting defiled food on My altar" (1:7)

Here began the first of three crucial issues raised in God's accusation against them—their unworthy acts of worship. "When you present a lame or sick animal, is it not wrong? Bring it to your governor. Would he be pleased with you or show you favor?" (1:8).

God had instructed them that sacrificed animals were to be healthy and free of all blemishes. "Any man of the house of Israel or of the foreign residents in Israel who presents his offering—whether they present freewill gifts or payment of vows to the LORD as burnt offerings—must offer an unblemished male from the cattle, sheep, or goats in order for you to be accepted. You are not to present anything that has a defect, because it will not be accepted on your behalf" (Lev. 22:18b–20). With tongue in cheek, Malachi suggested they try bringing inferior gifts like these to their governor, to someone they would actually have to look in the eye and be evaluated by in person. Would men be so audacious as to demean their leaders in this way?

I have actually had people indicate that they ignored their tithe but paid their taxes because they feared an audit by the Internal Revenue Service. Well, God may not come to your house yearly for an annual audit, but he does promise that there will be a *final* audit—"For indeed, the day is coming, burning like a furnace, when all the arrogant and everyone who commits wickedness will become stubble" (Mal. 4:1a).

Israel's sin—their "lip service"—was not supported by their "life service." The Lord looks at both the heart of the one bringing the offering and the purity of the gift. Our gifts of service today are polluted when we bring less than our best.

Recent data should cause us to look carefully at this. In 1933 American Protestants, clawing out a living in the depths of the Great Depression, gave 3.2 percent of their income through their churches. In 2001, when Americans were over *480 percent richer* after taxes and inflation than people during the Great Depression, Protestants gave only 2.7 percent of their income.[5]

Are we offering our best?

Second, Israel's failure to fear God in terms of appropriate worship had led to a downward moral spiral that impacted other areas of life. They were dealing treacherously with one another, in spite of the fact they all had the same heavenly Father who created them (2:10).

One aspect of their treachery was the profaning of their marriage vows. The family was under attack in Malachi's day, as it is in our own. The litany of sins sounds all too familiar—adultery, divorce, and marriage between believers and nonbelievers.

Their lack of spiritual discernment had led them to call evil good. "When you say, 'Everyone who does evil is good in the LORD's sight, and He is pleased with them'" (2:17b). Does that sound familiar? Our world is quickly moving toward relativism, and many Christians are reluctant to declare moral absolutes.

The next step in the downward moral spiral was to turn a blind eye to social ills. "I will come to you in judgment, and I will be ready to witness against sorcerers and adulterers; against those who swear falsely; against those who oppress the widow and the fatherless, and cheat the wage earner; and against those who deny justice to the foreigner" (3:5).

Does it surprise you that oppression of the needy is lumped in the same category with sorcerers and adulterers? It may. But these are all linked together with equal weight in God's litany of complaints against Israel's behavior. God is serious about his people using his resources by his standard for his glory. Why? The answer is simple but clear—"Because I, Yahweh, have not changed" (3:6).

The Day of His Coming

The first six verses of chapter 3 provide God's response to the question, "Where is the God of justice?" (2:17). But his answer was not what they expected. Many had come to believe that the "day of the Lord" was to be a panacea for all the ills of life, but God said their experience of the day of his coming would not be a pleasant one.

Dr. Kaiser writes, "They would learn firsthand that God was indeed just and that His justice would be observed in His preparation of the path by a forerunner (3:1a), His coming (3:1b–2), His refining work (3:3–4), His judgment (3:5), and His long-suffering (3:6).[6] To put his coming into bold relief, he asked two questions—"But who can endure the day of His coming? And who will be able to stand when He appears?" (3:2).

In contrast to the popular conception, God's coming will be like a refiner's fire and like cleansing lye. This phrase has become a familiar one to us from the refrain of Handel's *Messiah*. Fire separates slag from metal, just as soap separates dirt from clothes. Notice that the sons of Levi, the very people against whom the indictments in 1:6–2:9 had been levied, were singled out to be purified and refined like gold and silver (3:3). God's desire is to use this experience to purify, cleanse, and restore his people to productive living.

The Promise of Restoration

But how much better, the Lord says, if the fire doesn't have as much waste to consume, if the soap finds the body clean. So he held out a magnanimous offer—"'Return to Me, and I will return to you', says the LORD of Hosts" (3:7). This is simply a call for revival. *Return* is the Old Testament term for *repent*.

Once again, however, Israel responded to God's grace with a whine of innocence—"How can we return?" (3:7b). Their statement implied that they still didn't understand the gravity of their sin. They didn't understand that repentance begins with a change of heart, which results in a change of mind, which is demonstrated in a change of behavior. They were showing none of it.

Especially not in their giving.

Therefore, God took the opportunity to help them see what their lack of authenticity and generosity in giving was truly like, painting it in terms they had likely never considered but needed to see in stark detail—*they had stolen from the King*. The term *rob* is used in the Old Testament only here and in Proverbs 22:23. It means "to rob, defraud, or to overreach." In Talmudic literature it means "to take forcibly."[7]

We have already looked at the tithe in some detail. It was generally considered to be a tenth of what one earned and was intended to be brought to the storehouse. Stephen Olford wrote: "From the time of Hezekiah, there was in the sanctuary a storehouse built for depositing the tithes and

offerings of the people. This was also true of the second temple in the days
of Nehemiah."[8] They were to bring their tithes and offerings to the place
that God had chosen so that "there may be food in My house" (Mal. 3:10).
The giving of tithes and offerings was an opportunity to worship God and
participate in his work.

And when we don't, we do a lot more damage than we think.

When we rob God, we are actually cheating ourselves because it places
us under a curse (3:9) that closes the floodgates of God's blessing. This is
language we don't often use. We love to talk about "blessing." The idea of
"cursing" seems foreign to our ears.

Cursing obviously speaks of God's judgment for sin. We have two case
studies from the Bible where judgment for robbing God was swift and public. Achan robbed God of the gold of Jericho, which was designated for the
Lord's treasury (Josh. 6:18–19), and Ananias and Sapphira lied to the Holy
Spirit when they failed to fulfill their vow (Acts 5).

To understand the interplay between blessing and cursing, we should
look back at Deuteronomy 11:26–28a. "Look, today I set before you a blessing and a curse: there will be a blessing, if you obey the commands of the
Lord your God I am giving you today, and a curse, if you do not obey the
commands of the Lord your God." If blessing is defined in terms of God's
presence, provision, and protection, then cursing is the opposite of the same.
And as free moral agents, our obedience or lack thereof determines which
we receive from God's hand—blessing or cursing. Remember "cursing" is the
result of our volatile disobedience that removes us from God's protection.

Thus God issued a challenge—"Bring the full 10 percent into the storehouse. . . . Test Me in this way" (3:10).

The emphasis on the whole tithe may have been intended to emphasize
God's concern for the giving of man's entire being—time, talents, money,
influence—the giving of ourselves as a "living sacrifice." God indicated that
he would allow Israel to test him and see if their obedience made a difference. Notice that God promised three immediate results. He would (1) open
the floodgates of heaven and pour out a blessing, (2) rebuke the devourer,
and (3) ensure that the nations would consider them fortunate.

The first two images would have communicated more powerfully in
Malachi's day than they do our own. The opening of the floodgates of
heaven was an indication of an abundance of rain (Deut. 28:12), a blessing
that was prescribed to be "without measure." Their dependence on the rain
was much more acute than ours seems today.

The "devourer" probably referred to the dreaded locusts that could
quickly strip and eat away a crop. Do you ever feel like your life and resources

have dried up or are being consumed by a horde of locusts? If so, have you heeded God's warning about robbing from him? Do you have the faith to accept God's challenge?

The Greatest Promise

Don't miss the final promise: "'Then all the nations will consider you fortunate, for you will be a delightful land,' says the LORD of Hosts" (v. 12). This reminds us of the promise made to Abram in Genesis 12:2. But this is not the first mention of the nations in the book of Malachi.

Three times in the opening chapter, God repeated a promise that is at the heart of his reason for offering blessing. "'For My name will be great among the nations, from the rising of the sun to its setting. Incense and pure offerings will be presented in My name in every place because My name will be great among the nations,' says the LORD of Hosts. . . . 'For I am a great King,' says the LORD of Hosts, 'and My name will be feared among the nations'" (Mal. 1:11, 14).

God's heartbeat to open the windows, pour out blessing, and rebuke the devourer has to do with his singular passion to be known as King among all the nations. It's not just about us. It's not about us getting our own personal windfall. That may happen, and that will be fine.

But never forget, we receive blessing to become a blessing, to further our role in God's great and glorious kingdom work.

Living in the Kingdom Zone

But seek first the kingdom of God and His righteousness,
and all these things will be provided for you.

MATTHEW 6:33

This became my life verse one year when I attended a Fellowship of Christian Athlete's camp in Black Mountain, North Carolina. I had just been awarded a scholarship to play football at Wake Forest, and the chance to work out with several professional athletes was too good to miss. Memories of those workouts have long since faded, but the testimonies of the men who were there still seem vibrant. Throughout the week this verse seemed to be a central feature, and it has been a key theme for me ever since.

Athletes often speak of being in the "zone." Generally it means that their game has moved to another level where high-level performance is accomplished with apparent ease.

We remember how Michael Jordan would get in a zone and every shot seemed to find nothing but net. Peyton Manning is a quarterback who often gets in the zone and completes pass after pass.

What would it be like to live in the "kingdom zone"? How do we get there?

Three Kingdom Principles

Hopefully, you have had the chance to read my earlier book *Empowering Kingdom Growth: The Heartbeat of God*, or perhaps you have worked through the study by that name. If so, this section will refresh your memory. If not, this may encourage you to participate in that original study.

Three themes run throughout Scripture concerning the kingdom zone. God is looking for a people who will:

- embody his name,
- embrace his mission to the nations,
- and obey his Word.

We find this in the covenant promise recorded in Exodus 19:5-6. "Now if you will listen to Me and carefully keep My covenant, you will be My own possession out of all the peoples, although all the earth is Mine, and you will be My kingdom of priests and My holy nation."

God's name represents his character, and Israel's holy behavior was mandated because they represented a holy King. Israel was chosen to join the King in reclaiming the earth, which is rightfully his. But to be effective in this task, it was critical that they obey his Word. If so—if they were willing to track with his heartbeat—God promised that he would bless them in such abundance that they would have the resources to accomplish their kingdom responsibilities.

Ezekiel 36 records the "agony and ecstasy" of the Old Testament. Israel had suffered a humiliating defeat and was now languishing in Babylonian captivity. The prophet told them that they had profaned God's name (v. 20), that they had *consumed* God's blessing and had not *conveyed* it.

But Ezekiel issued a clarion note of hope: "The nations will know that I am Yahweh—the declaration of the Lord GOD—when I demonstrate My holiness through you in their sight" (36:23b). If you read Ezekiel 36 carefully, you will find multiple references to fruitful and abundant provision with a singular focus—the reaching of the nations.

We then begin the New Testament with this stark announcement: "Repent, because the kingdom of heaven has come near!" (Matt. 3:2). The focal point of Jesus' life and ministry was the kingdom. Does it surprise you, in fact, that the first three statements in the prayer of Jesus (Matt. 6:9–13) pick up the three kingdom themes of the Old Testament?

- "Your name be honored as holy." This means embodying his name!
- "Your kingdom come." This means embracing his mission!
- "Your will be done." This means obeying his Word!

The community of believers that would soon become the New Testament church were chosen, then, to complete and fulfill God's kingdom mission. He promised to give them "the keys of the kingdom." And he promised them resources to accomplish the task he was building (Matt. 16:19).

We have been called to a supernatural work that requires us to rely on the Holy Spirit and employ all of God's resources with his heartbeat in mind. We must learn to live in the kingdom zone because we are *God's resources* to accomplish his kingdom purposes.

The Promise of Adequate Provision

Moving deeper into the Lord's Prayer, we come across three clauses of kingdom provision that balance and give grounds for pursuing our kingdom commitments. Daily bread, forgiveness of sin, and deliverance from evil assure the kingdom citizen that everything necessary to live in the kingdom zone has been provided. "Our requests for daily bread, forgiveness of sins, and deliverance from evil are not selfish demands; instead they are understood requirements for serving in His kingdom."[9]

Our material needs are represented by "daily bread." It is not unlikely that the promise of "daily bread" would have reminded these early Jewish believers of God's miraculous provision for Israel years before through the daily showers of manna. But this request continues to serve as a constant reminder that our everyday life and the kingdom are inextricably bound together. It also assures us that we will have sufficient resources to accomplish the task he has given us in the advancing of his kingdom.

Therefore, I have used the benediction of this prayer to formulate my life's goal—"I will advance his kingdom by his power for his glory!" Will you join me in doing that?

Collecting Treasures in Heaven

Treasure hunting is a childhood fascination for many and a life's work for others. But Jesus said that it is possible to live in such a manner that you can "collect for yourselves treasures in heaven" (6:20).

Treasures in heaven are contrasted with treasures on earth. Earthly treasures provide neither security nor satisfaction. They are always susceptible to moth, rust, and thieves. Much of the wealth of first-century persons was in costly garments that could be consumed by moths. Metal treasure can rust, and thieves can take any and all of those things we collect. This fact alone can result in undue anxiety, robbing our joy and keeping us from focusing on God's kingdom. Material possessions are good servants but poor masters. Materialism will enslave the heart and render us ineffective in terms of kingdom service.

The larger danger with earthly treasure, however, is laid out in verse 21. "For where your treasure is, there your heart will be also." The issue is not the level of our *wealth* but the level of our *loyalty*. The danger inherent in amassing earthly treasure is that our treasure will ultimately command our loyalty. Material affluence can easily breed materialism.

Is it any wonder that, immediately following the encounter with the rich young ruler, Jesus warned his followers; "I assure you: It will be hard for a rich person to enter the kingdom of heaven" (Matt. 19:23). Paul would later exhort young Timothy to instruct the rich not to put their trust in riches but on God who provides us with all things. How can they do this? "Instruct them to do good, to be rich in good works, to be generous, willing to share" (1 Tim. 6:18). The lure of wealth is subtle indeed.

So we have another option—using our God-given resources to lay up treasure in heaven. Treasures in heaven are stored up by obedience to God in all areas of our lives as we use our time, talents, influence, and money to advance God's kingdom "on earth as it is in heaven."

In Matthew 19, Jesus instructed the rich young ruler that he could have "treasure in heaven" by selling his possessions and giving to the poor (v. 21). Paul counseled Timothy to tell those with abundant material resources that when they were generous and willing to share, they would store up "a good foundation for the age to come, so that they may take hold of life that is real" (1 Tim. 6:19). When we give money or time and talents to share the gospel with the nations, we are laying up treasure in heaven.

"Do you see the connection here, though? We store treasure in heaven by giving to needy *people*, by doing good works for other *people*, by support-ing mission causes that take the gospel to unsaved *people*."[10] Compare this with what we learned about the purposes of material resources in our Old Testament study. It's simple—*we lay up kingdom treasures when we live our lives with kingdom focus.*

The illustration of the eye (6:22–23) may strike us as odd, but it would have been clear to the early disciples. The eye was the lamp of the body in the sense that it enabled the body to find its way. But for the eye to be an effective guide, it must be "complete" or "sound." "So the 'single eye' is pri-marily a metaphor for a life totally devoted to the service of God. But *haplotes* (sound) is also used in the New Testament with a connotation of generosity." The "evil eye" was a regular expression to denote jealousy and cheapness.[11]

The generous person has a clear eye while the stingy person has an evil eye. The eye focused on evil draws us into evil ways and away from kingdom focus. The idea expressed here is on a purposeful life, a life directed toward its true purpose—the kingdom of God.

Jesus went on to remind us that no one can be a slave of two masters. We might have two employers, but we can never have two masters. *Hate* may seem like a strong term, but often in Scripture it carries a comparative sense. It does not so much mean "active dislike" but rather "displacement by a higher loyalty."

Are you devoted to money, or are you devoted to the kingdom? Are you serving money, or is your money serving God? How would your checkbook bear witness to your answer?

Life in the Kingdom Zone

Kingdom citizens can live in the zone to such an extent that life is freed from anxiety. Jesus commanded his followers, "Don't worry about your life." He addressed two principle concerns of earthly life—food and clothing—as areas where we could experience anxiety-free living. His illustrations were drawn from nature—birds and wildflowers. Neither of them toils anxiously, and yet God provides for their every need.

Granted, these illustrations do not rule out responsible concern or everyday things, nor do they suggest that we shouldn't work. But kingdom people do not press life. They allow God to provide it.

So Jesus asked a simple question: "If that's how God clothes the grass of the field, which is here today and thrown into the furnace tomorrow, won't He do much more for you—you of little faith?" (Matt. 6:30). "Little faith" is used frequently in Matthew's Gospel (8:26; 14:31; 16:8; 17:20) to describe disciples who fail to trust Jesus for provision. If disciples can trust God for eternal security, why should they exhibit such little faith when it comes to daily living? To live with undue anxiety is to live like a pagan who believes that every provision of life is his own doing (6:32).

Jesus gave us the key to living in the kingdom zone—"But seek first the kingdom of God and His righteousness, and all these things will be provided for you" (v. 33). "Seek" translates a present imperative verb, and thus it means that we consistently and persistently focus on the kingdom.

The kingdom citizen is submissive to his will here and now and focused on advancing his kingdom as a first priority of life.

The kingdom citizen also accepts God's principles about the management of his resources, knowing that God's desire is to provide abundantly for those who have his heartbeat and demonstrate it by using all their material resources to advance his kingdom.

So you can begin to seek his kingdom by presenting yourself and all you have to him right now, this very minute. Ask him to show you where he is advancing his kingdom today and how you can participate. Look for opportunities to share your faith. Look for opportunities to give beyond the tithe.

Look for a life only he can provide but one that will make any other seem shallow and wasteful by comparison.

Let's start using our money to seek his kingdom.

Good Reasons to Be a Giver

Week 5, Day 1

Developing Consistency

*On the first day of the week, each of you is to set something aside
and save to the extent that he prospers, so that no collections
will need to be made when I come.*

1 CORINTHIANS 16:2

When I was at Southwestern Seminary, I had the joy of teaching 1 Corinthians. I would often begin the lecture with a statement and a question, "The church at Corinth is looking for a new pastor. Would any of you like for me to send your resume?" The response was usually muffled chuckles.

If you have read the Corinthian letters, you know that the church there was anything but boring. They were awash with church cliques, immoral behavior, jealousy over leaders and former leaders, lawsuits among members, uncertainty over the use of spiritual gifts, and doctrinal confusion.

I know what you may be thinking! Sounds a little like what we see in churches today.

Throughout this week we will be looking at several passages in both of the Corinthian letters that deal specifically with stewardship as practiced by the early church. As we study these passages together, keep in mind that "all Scripture is inspired by God and is profitable for teaching, for rebuking, for correcting, for training in righteousness, so that the man of God may be complete, equipped for every good work" (2 Tim. 3:16–17).

Ask the Father to show you what will make you complete.

Excel in the Lord's Work

One area of theological confusion in the Corinthian church related to the resurrection of believers, but Paul's response in 1 Corinthians 15 is one of the greatest declarations of the truth and impact of the resurrection ever composed.

He began by listing the eyewitnesses, "most of whom remain to the present" (v. 6). In other words, he challenged any skeptic to look at the evidence. He forced his readers to ask themselves, "What if Christ had not been raised?"

I have used this question on numerous occasions to witness to skeptics. The ramifications are too horrifying to mention. Our faith would be in vain, there would be no forgiveness for sins, and every person who has died would have simply perished with no hope of eternity.

Paul responded in thunder: "But now Christ *has* been raised from the dead, the firstfruits of those who have fallen asleep" (15:20); then followed his bold declaration by giving us a glimpse of the resurrection body, using words like *incorruption, glory, power,* and *spiritual* to describe the indescribable (vv. 42–44). Truly, the reality of the resurrection has altered everything forever for kingdom citizens, because "flesh and blood cannot inherit the kingdom of God" (v. 50a).

We can't afford to let Paul's arguments descend into a mere doctrinal discussion. As we have previously noted, doctrine should never be taught simply to satisfy our curiosity. That's why to summarize his teaching, Paul added a *therefore*: "Therefore, my dear brothers, be steadfast, immovable, always excelling in the Lord's work, knowing that your labor in the Lord is not in vain" (15:58).

The Corinthian believers were prone to fickleness, both in their loyalties and in their service—like we can be. But when we get a clear picture of the death and resurrection and an understanding of the empowering available to the believer, we will not be easily shaken. We will be "steadfast" and "immovable," as Paul encouraged the Corinthians to be. Rock solid.

And something more: We, like the Corinthians before us, are to demonstrate our kingdom resolve by "excelling in the Lord's work" (v. 58).

This phrase could be taken to mean that all we do is "the Lord's work." This sounds impossible and highly impractical in one sense, and yet it is certainly true. We have been guilty of compartmentalizing our life in terms of sacred and secular. But for the kingdom citizen, *nothing* is secular. Every aspect of our life comes under the sovereign rule of the King. Yet "the Lord's work" may also mean a specific ministry accomplished for the Lord.

Every kingdom citizen is called, gifted, and empowered for ministry. There are no kingdom spectators.

Paul ended this section with a declaration that should encourage every one of us—"your labor in the Lord is not in vain." Do you ever feel that your life is passing you by with little if any purpose? Paul has some really good news for you—*the resurrection altered everything.* It assures us of God's ultimate triumph. For that reason our hard labor is "in the Lord" and therefore will never be empty or cast aside.

What do you do that impacts the kingdom and will last forever?

Now Concerning the Collection

In the original manuscript of 1 Corinthians, there was no break between chapters 15 and 16. Therefore, Paul's teaching on the power of the resurrection had a direct bearing on one particular labor in which he wanted them to remain steadfast and assured that it had kingdom significance. Stephen Olford, commenting on the connection between the resurrection and our opportunity to give, wrote, "In other words, the Lord Jesus gave Himself in death and resurrection, not in order to save us from sacrifice, but rather to teach us how to give ourselves and our substance in continual sacrifice."[1]

The phrase "now about" or "now concerning" is used five times in 1 Corinthians to signify questions the Corinthians had included in a letter sent to Paul (note especially 7:1). In each case, there existed some confusion in the minds of the Corinthians about the topic under discussion.

The issue in our present passage is the "collection for the saints" (1 Cor. 16:1). This collection was for the poor in Jerusalem, whose need had been made more acute by a famine. Paul was rallying the Gentile churches to support the brethren in Jerusalem, and it seems likely that the Corinthian church was lagging behind in their giving to this need.

So in his brief note of encouragement in chapter 16, we can discover several important principles of stewardship.

1. *The principle of consistency.* "On the first day of the week" (v. 2) provides the first evidence that first-century Christians worshipped together on the first day as a weekly celebration of the resurrection of the Lord (cp. John 20:19; Acts 20:7; and Rev. 1:10). Paul instructed them that on every first day, "each of you is to set something aside."

One characteristic of God is his consistency and orderliness. Earlier in chapter 14, Paul corrected certain practices of worship by insisting that God is not a God of disorder but of peace (v. 33). Thus Paul's final instruction about worship speaks to order and consistency, as well: "But everything must be done decently and in order" (v. 40). If the Corinthians would consistently set aside their offering on the first day, no collections would need to be made when Paul arrived. In other words, Paul wanted them to give generously and regularly so they would be giving from the heart and not because of pressure that may have been exerted by his presence.

Our giving should be a matter of theological conviction that leads to practical and consistent expression. Consistency requires thought, planning, and preparation that in turn allows us to have a greater sense of worship as we give.

I can still remember my parents giving me money and an offering envelope every Sunday. This principle of consistency became so engrained in me; it was second nature. I would no more have thought about going to church without an offering than I would have gone to school without my books or out to play baseball without a glove.

When my wife and I had children, we also had the privilege of teaching them how to worship with their tithes and offerings. We would give them their allowance in such a fashion that it was easy to calculate the tithe. We made sure they had their envelopes prepared before Sunday morning.

These lessons stick. My daughter Rachael was once given a college assignment to develop a budget based on a fictional salary. She felt like she had done well on the assignment because she was able to balance income and expenditures with money left for savings, but her paper was returned with a low grade. When she inquired about it, the professor told her and the entire class it was unrealistic to place a 10 percent gift to the church first in her budget. With such a small income, she couldn't afford such generosity. She calmly responded, "My father always taught me that 90 percent with God is better than 100 percent without him." Talk about a proud father! It has been a joy to see that my children have grown up to be good managers of money.

I have known few generous givers who were not first consistent givers. What can you do to develop consistency? First, I would suggest that you follow Paul's direction about laying aside your tithe and offering first. When you sit down to write your checks for the week, write this one first. If your church provides an envelope, put your check in it the day you write it and place it in your Bible. By following a consistent procedure, you will arrive prepared to worship through your consecrated gifts and offerings.

2. *The principle of personal responsibility.* The phrase "each of you" means exactly what it says. No one is to be excluded. Rich and poor, old and young, male and female—each one is given the privilege and responsibility to participate in this offering. In 2 Corinthians 8:2, in fact, Paul told them that the churches of Macedonia gave generously out of their deep poverty.

Giving is essentially personal because God associates the gift with the giver. "Money has no value whatsoever, unless it is the expression of life, labor and love. Furthermore, God has no favorites in his purpose of blessing, and since He wants to bless everyone, He expects everyone to give."[2] No one should ever be excluded from worshipping God through tithes and offerings, and no one should do so without theological reflection that leads to thoughtfulness and consistency.

3. *The principle of proportionate giving.* Paul didn't specify a certain amount in this text. Having been nurtured in Judaism, Paul would have practiced tithing according to Old Testament prescriptions. But in this case Paul simply stated that each person should give "to the extent that he prospers."

The New International Version translates this phrase "in keeping with his income" (1 Cor. 16:2), but that reflects too much of our present culture. Some of the early Christians were slaves who had little or no income. Some Jews when they became Christians were ostracized by their families, and thus they were often dependent on the church for support. Remember, however, that Paul had already underlined the necessity for "each one" to participate.

By giving them the opportunity to give "to the extent that he prospers" (1 Cor. 16:2), some would have the opportunity to give larger gifts than others, thus ensuring that the collection would be sufficient to meet the needs of the saints in Jerusalem. There can be little question that Paul anticipated this offering would be a generous one. In verses 3 and 4, he spoke to the issue of transporting this gift to Jerusalem.

Proportionate giving requires us first to consider the extent of our blessings. *And I don't think Paul was referring only to financial blessing!* Remember the linking of this text to the teaching of the resurrection. In Ephesians 1:3, Paul declared that God has "blessed us with every spiritual blessing in the heavens, in Christ." Proportionate giving comes from the overflow that recognizes God as the source of life and the owner of everything, and thus all that we have comes from his hand.

Proportionate giving requires us seriously to consider what we give to God. I assume you have probably surmised that this offering was in addition to the normal giving for the needs of the church in Corinth. Thus, in the giving of this additional offering, Paul encouraged them to consider the blessings of the Lord before they decided on what they would give.

In one of our many building campaigns in Norfolk, we invited the congregation to make a gift beyond the tithe for the children's wing. My daughter Tina was old enough to understand that we were asking for a special offering, and she wanted to participate. So we sat down at the table to consider what would be an appropriate gift beyond her tithe.

We had challenged the people to consider a percentage gift, which makes the gift proportionate. And after she had determined what she would give, she asked what I planned to give. When I told her, she then wanted to know how much I made. When I told her, she simply responded, "Daddy, that's not fair; you will have more left." But even after patiently explaining to her that I had significantly more bills to pay than she did, I had to think once again about what I had determined to give.

Was it enough? Was it proportional? Did it have a kingdom mentality and conviction behind it?

Have you ever looked at your checkbook after you write your check for your tithes and offerings to see how much God has let you keep? How deeply and richly and generously have you been blessed by God, not just financially but in every other way?

How does your giving stack up to these biblical ideals?

The Grace of Giving

During a severe testing by affliction, their abundance of joy and their deep poverty overflowed into the wealth of their generosity.

2 Corinthians 8:2

The story goes that a man was attending a cattle auction where the auctioneer was enumerating the qualities of a beautiful Guernsey cow. The newcomer, eager to buy the cow, asked an old farmer who seemed to know something about every cow at the auction, "How much does she give?" The old-timer responded, "Doesn't give a thing, but if you can get her in a corner, you can take a lot from her."

I am afraid this has been the experience of many believers who have never developed the grace of giving or discovered the joy of giving. They have been backed into a corner with emotional pitches lathered with guilt.

If that's been your experience, you have a treat in store for you when you develop the grace of giving.

Overflowing with Generosity

As we begin looking into the second letter to the Corinthians, we find that it has been a year, or perhaps somewhat less, since Paul had given them instructions for the giving to the collection for the saints in Jerusalem (1 Cor. 16:1–4). And during that year Paul had been forced to write a painful letter (2 Cor. 7:8) that had grieved the Corinthians. This letter had positive results, however, and Paul rejoiced that they had repented (7:9). So with the church restored to health, Paul now devoted virtually two chapters to the grace of giving (chapters 8–9). These chapters contain principles that are applicable to Christians of every age.

The churches in Macedonia were further along in their participation in the offering than the church in Corinth was. Therefore, Paul used them as an example to stimulate the Corinthians to complete their offering (8:11). Macedonia included all the districts of Greece north of the Isthmus of Corinth. Its churches would have included Philippi, Thessalonica, and Berea. The fact that these churches had given generously to this offering, added to the teaching here in 2 Corinthians, indicates that whenever Paul planted a church, he taught them the principles of generous stewardship.

The generous giving of the churches in Macedonia is made all the more exemplary because "their abundance of joy and their deep poverty overflowed into the wealth of their generosity" (v. 2).

The believers in Macedonia were both poor and persecuted. C. K. Barrett suggests that their poverty was the result of persecution for their faith. "*Poverty* was probably to a great extent a Christian phenomenon and the result of persecution, for Macedonia seems on the whole to have been a prosperous province, with flourishing agriculture and mining and lumbering industries."[3] I have always found it curious that people with little means are often more generous than those with great abundance. Does accumulation of wealth make us more dependent on wealth for our security?

Joy and *generosity* are twins. When you discover one in the life of a person, you can expect to find the other. Joy comes from the knowledge of sins forgiven and the contemplation of God's generosity on our behalf. It is not deterred by one's circumstances, even if those circumstances include "severe testing by affliction" (v. 2). Joy thus leads one to generosity, and generosity in turn gives one great joy. "Generosity" indicates giving that both uncalculating and unpretentious, free from human motivation. Miserly people are *miserable* people, and generous people are *joyous*.

Paul could thus declare that the generosity of the Macedonians was a visible expression of divine grace. The word *grace* actually means "generosity." It is the generosity of God that freely gives sinners what they don't deserve and couldn't afford—forgiveness. The use of *grace* here, however, doesn't simply mean that their offering was *motivated* by grace. It goes beyond that to suggest that it was an *act* of grace.

In other words, their giving was made possible by the empowering of the Holy Spirit. The Spirit had enabled them to give more than their means appeared to warrant. The Spirit prompted them to give to people they had never seen simply because those in need were members of the same body.

The Corinthians, we know, had demonstrated their zeal for "matters of the Spirit" in their quest to possess the more spectacular gifts that often drew attention to the person possessing the gift. Paul had attempted to redirect this zeal in 1 Corinthians 14:12 by encouraging them to seek to abound for the building up of the church. In our present passage, Paul declared that the generous giving of the Macedonian churches was as much a demonstration of the Spirit as prophecy or miracle-working faith.

Do you give from God's abundance or from your own resources? If you want to discover true joy, allow the Holy Spirit to empower your giving.

Grace Giving Begins with "You"

Paul shared the key to "grace giving" in verse 5. "Instead, they gave themselves especially to the Lord, then to us by God's will." Thus, grace giving begins with the offering of ourselves to the Lord.

We looked briefly at this principle in our study of Romans 12:1–2. Perhaps, though, you are wondering what distinguishes "grace giving" from other, lesser forms of generosity. According to Paul it has four unique characteristics:

1. *Grace giving is spontaneous.* Paul testified that the churches in Macedonia chose to participate in this offering "on their own" (8:3). In other words, Paul exerted no pressure to convince them to give. In the light of their poverty, it's possible that Paul had been reluctant to mention the offering to them, not wanting to overburden them. But their passion to give was so directed by the Spirit that Paul indicates, "They begged us insistently" (v. 4). When we discover the grace of giving, no one will have to back us into the corner and browbeat us into giving. We will insist that we be allowed to give.

One of the great joys of being president of Southwestern Seminary was the opportunity to meet people who were donors to the school. One thing that stands out clearly in my memory is meeting those who give with such joy and abandon. They made me feel that I had done them a great service by allowing them to participate in the ministry of the school.

2. *Grace giving is beyond our ability.* Paul declared that the Christians in the church of Macedonia gave "according to their ability and beyond

their ability" (v. 3). Grace giving allows us to move beyond "proportionate giving" to "supernatural giving."

During one of our building programs at First Norfolk, I was invited by one of our senior adults to join her for lunch in her retirement home. It was a humble place, and the furnishings were sparse. After lunch she asked me to read a passage of Scripture and quickly handed me her Bible. When I opened to the requested text, I found a financial gift that was clearly beyond her ability. I nearly offended her when I insisted that the gift would be too great a sacrifice for someone on a limited income. But this was what she had decided, and she gave me a lesson in grace giving.

3. *Grace giving sees the privilege of sharing in ministry.* The Macedonian believers simply would not be deprived of the privilege of sharing in the ministry to the saints.

Paul pulled together two unique words in describing these churches' stewardship that are somewhat obscured by our English translations. First, the word translated "privilege" or "favor" is actually the word *charis* in the Greek. This word is normally translated "grace" and is the root of the word *charismata*, which Paul used to describe "gifts of the Spirit." Both the ability and the desire to give were produced in the Macedonian believers by the Holy Spirit, every bit as much as the more flowery spiritual gifts were.

The second word is *koinonia*, which is often translated as "fellowship." In 1 Corinthians 1:9, Paul used the same term to speak of our relationship with Christ as "fellowship with His Son." In Galatians 2:9, it is used in terms of *human* fellowship, when Paul recounted the pillars of the faith giving him their right hand of fellowship. The word can also mean "generosity" (2 Cor. 9:13) or even "a contribution" (Rom. 15:26).

It is worth our time to look at Romans 15:26 at this point, which confirms that "Macedonia and Achaia were pleased to make a contribution to the poor among the saints in Jerusalem." This tells us that fellowship flows from our relationship with the Son, creates a bond of community, and is evidenced in our generous response to the needs of the family. Fellowship is more than a warm embrace and a shared meal; it is shared life.

The word translated ministry is *diakonia*, from which we derive our English word *deacon*. The Macedonian believers saw giving to this collection as an opportunity to share in ministry. When you give an offering through your church, do you celebrate the truth that you are sharing in ministry? Do you know and pray for the ministries and ministers you help support through your church and denomination?

4. *Grace giving begins with "me."* The Macedonians had gone beyond what Paul had dared hope in the sense that "they gave themselves especially

to the Lord, then to us by God's will" (2 Cor. 8:5). Apparently they had volunteered to help Paul in any way possible.

All giving stems from the offering of ourselves to the Lord as living sacrifices (Rom. 12:1). But such an offering will always find practical expression. When we have truthfully offered ourselves to Christ, we will ultimately offer ourselves in service.

The giving of our tithes and offerings through our local church does not exempt us from the call to serve. It seems apparent that many believers would rather give their offerings in order to pay someone else to serve than to roll up their sleeves and do the work of ministry. The old adage about 20 percent of the membership doing 80 percent of the work must be challenged and overturned if we are serious about advancing God's kingdom.

Grace Giving Defines Great Churches

Paul had been so encouraged by the generosity of the Macedonians that he urged Titus to return to Corinth "so he should also complete this grace to you" (2 Cor. 8:6). Again, Paul referred to this collection with the simple term "grace."

But Paul then moved beyond an appeal based on the example of the Macedonian churches, reminding the Corinthians of the spiritual resources available to them.

This verse is reminiscent of 1 Corinthians 1:4–5: "I always thank my God for you because of God's grace given to you in Christ Jesus, that by Him you were made rich in everything—in all speaking and all knowledge." The Corinthians were proud of the abundance of spiritual gifts they possessed, and they boasted that they excelled in gifts of miracle-working faith, utterance, and knowledge, which they believed gave them insight into mysteries of the faith. In 1 Corinthians, Paul had attempted to cure their spiritual pride and focus them on seeking gifts that edified the whole body. This time he simply used their pride in spiritual gifts to motivate them to "excel also in this grace" (2 Cor. 8:7). Generous giving is as much a divine gift as is prophecy.

In verses 8–15, Paul declared that grace giving demonstrates the genuineness of love. He used Christ as his supreme example, who "although He was rich, for your sake He became poor, so that by His poverty you might become rich" (v. 9).

"Became poor" translates an aorist tense suggesting it is a reference to the incarnation. For us to become rich, the King of glory took upon himself the role of a suffering servant. Luke 9:58 describes him as one who had no place to lay his head. The King died without a single possession. Even his garments were stripped from his body. He was buried in a borrowed tomb. He became poor to make us rich in grace.

But Jesus performed this act of self-giving so that we might be forgiven and one day share in his glory. Did you notice that Paul insisted he was not saying this as a command (v. 8) but rather was giving an opinion that would be profitable for them (v. 10)? When one fully comprehends the grace made available in the self-sacrifice of Christ, no command to give ought to be necessary.

Jesus, of course—as we saw earlier—had approached tithing from the perspective of an assumed truth, as something that God's people should already have mastered without neglecting the weightier things like love, mercy, and justice. In other words, Jesus was saying, "I shouldn't have to go back and cover elementary school matters with you."

Paul, too, was clear in saying that the tithe was only the beginning of Christian stewardship. In 1 Corinthians 16 he taught systematic giving. He then went beyond that to teach joyful, cheerful, or hilarious giving. I hear some people say you ought to give until it hurts. Paul would say you need to give until it becomes fun.

But finally he went beyond that to the "grace giving" we've been talking about—supernatural giving. He challenged them to grow in their stewardship to the point that they were giving at a level where they were depending on the Lord to supply the seed.

The phrase "for you know the grace of our Lord Jesus Christ" (v. 9) speaks of personal knowledge. If they had experienced grace—if they were Christians at all—then giving should flow from their innermost being. What may have been a moral duty for Old Testament man had now become a joyous privilege produced in the believer by the Holy Spirit.

It still is today.

Paul concluded with an appeal both to proportionate and generous giving (v. 12). Their surplus would enable them to meet the present need of the saints who were suffering in Jerusalem (v. 14). But one day the tables may be reversed, he said, and the believers in Jerusalem may have the opportunity to share with them.

We often define great churches by their size or by the giftedness of the pastor and people. The Corinthian church had considered themselves a great church because of the abundance of spiritual gifts possessed by the members. But Paul challenged them to be a great church in terms of generosity.

That's a sure sign that something valuable is happening there—something of kingdom proportions.

As a pastor, I have seen church members give in this supernatural manner during a building campaign or special offering. In every instance the people who take such a challenge return with stories of supernatural provision and unusual spiritual growth. I wonder why we don't make this a regular practice? What would it be like to give this way for the reaching of the nations?

When I moved from Norfolk to work at the North American Mission Board, I joined First Baptist Church in Woodstock, Georgia. The church had just relocated and was experiencing tremendous growth.

I marveled as our pastor Johnny Hunt invited the church to give to a special need on such a regular basis that it seemed like a weekly occurrence. One Wednesday evening in particular, I remember we gave enough to buy a vehicle for a missionary. All of this was done apart from the regular tithes and gifts to the building fund.

I once remarked to my wife, "You just can't go to the well this often." But was I ever wrong! I learned from my pastor that the well is infinitely deep and that our greatest mistake is asking our people for too little. You may have heard about the great numerical growth of First Baptist Church in Woodstock, but you may not know that its greatness flows from a generous heart that reflects God's heartbeat for the world.

Your church can do the same—no matter how small your budget, no matter how hard the times, no matter how you've done things in the past.

Pursue greatness. Pursue grace. Pursue giving.

The Laws of Giving

Remember this: the person who sows sparingly will also reap sparingly, and the person who sows generously will also reap generously.

2 CORINTHIANS 9:6

When we moved to the Norfolk area, we purchased a home with a small but potentially lovely front yard. I was a poor pastor with two children, and thus I sprinkled the grass seed sparingly in the front yard.

Needless to say, my dream of a plush green lawn was dashed. My lawn looked more like a man with thinning hair and a poor comb-over.

My dad, who had quite the green thumb, told me that seed was inexpensive and that I should spread it liberally. So the next time I poured about fifty pounds of seed on my postage-stamp-sized yard. I may have overdone it, but I had a lush green yard the next spring.

This taught me a good lesson: If you expect to reap a big harvest, it helps to sow a lot of seed. In fact, it's a requirement.

Generosity Begets Generosity

Yesterday we looked at 2 Corinthians 8, Paul's teaching on developing the grace of giving. From 2 Corinthians 8:16 through 9:5, Paul gave additional details for how the collection of gifts was to be used for the aid of the saints in Jerusalem. We'll look at that today, as well as in the chapters that follow for this week.

In chapter 9, Paul indicated that the Corinthians knew enough about the need and plans for the offering that it was unnecessary to write anything additional about it. He knew of the Corinthians' eagerness to participate, and thus during his stay in Macedonia, he had shared this good news with the churches of Macedonia. Paul knew that *generosity begets generosity.* He gave them full credit for their readiness. Paul was in the habit of seeing the best in his people and telling that story to others.

Paul had sent Titus and two other brothers (8:16–18) to administrate the offering (9:3). It appears that Paul was himself planning a visit and anticipated that some of the Macedonian believers might accompany him (9:3b–4). Paul thus encouraged them to complete the task of receiving the offering. He didn't want either himself or the Corinthians to be embarrassed when their fellow believers arrived.

The word translated "generous gift" in verse 5 is from the Greek word *eulogia*, from which we get the English word *eulogy*. We sometimes forget that our giving is a "eulogy" or blessing to others. We often pray that God will bless someone, but we forget that we can also bestow a blessing on them by our own actions of giving.

If you want God to bless the poor, give to the poor.

If you want him to bless the missionaries, give to mission causes.

The directions that the Corinthians arrange their giving "in advance" (v. 5) reminds us of Paul's instructions in 1 Corinthians 16:2 where he stated that on the first day of the week they should "set something aside and save." Their giving was to be not only generous but also deliberate. Intentionality and generosity will guard us from a "covetousness" spirit that reduces our gift from a spontaneous act to a grudging offering.

So to encourage the Corinthians to complete the task, Paul articulated four laws of giving that are largely taken from an agricultural model. Let's look at them one at a time.

The Law of Sowing

Paul set forth a proposition that he knew they would both understand and accept as true—the law of sowing and reaping.

All other things being equal, the quantity of the harvest will always be proportionate to the quantity of seed sown. This is not a motive for giving; it is simply a by-product of sowing.

This same principle is taught with slightly different images by the writer of Proverbs. "One person gives freely, yet gains more; another withholds what is right, only to become poor. A generous person will be enriched, and the one who gives a drink of water will receive water" (11:24–25). "Kindness to the poor is a loan to the LORD, and He will give a reward to the lender" (19:17).

Isn't this the essence of what Jesus taught in Luke 6:38? "Give, and it will be given to you; a good measure—pressed down, shaken together, and running over—will be poured into your lap. For with the measure you use, it will be measured back to you."

Paul wanted the Corinthians to understand that their giving to the saints in Jerusalem was a form of sowing that would be followed by a rich harvest of blessing. The generous giver need not fear destitution. In a real sense, a generous person receives far more than he gives.

One year the Hemphill family decided to buy Christmas gifts for a needy family who had several children and lived near us on the seminary campus. We surprised them with the gifts they were not expecting. I had more fun watching Katie, our youngest, laugh with delight as the children opened their gifts.

It's true—you always receive more than you sow.

The Law of Cheerful Giving

Paul declared, "Each person should do as he has decided in his heart" (2 Cor. 9:7). Giving is the outward expression of inner conviction. Thus, cheerful giving is not motivated by praise or the fear of censure. As Paul said, it is "not out of regret or out of necessity" (v. 7).

The phrase "out of regret" speaks of giving grudgingly, as if one is reluctant to part with what he considers to be his own. "Out of necessity" probably has in mind the person who is afraid of what others may think if he doesn't give. It's obvious that such motives rob the giver of the joy God intends him to experience.

The bottom line for Paul was that "God loves a cheerful giver" (v. 7). This may be an adaptation of Proverbs 22:9: "A generous person will be blessed." The word *love* here should be understood in terms of "approves" or "rewards." This does not suggest that God doesn't love those who fail to give generously. We know that God loved us even while we were ungodly. The point is that God, who is by nature a giver, loves to see his children display his character. Isn't it awesome that God wants us to enjoy giving in service to him? What a pity the Pharisees who tithed mint, dill, and cumin missed the joy of knowing and serving a God who loves.

What a pity when we do, as well.

The Law of Sufficiency

It is a tragedy that many Christians live their lives as if their spiritual resources might run out. We give sparingly, afraid that we might not have enough. We fail to volunteer because we just don't have the time. We refuse to forgive, thinking we must do it based on our own ability to produce forgiveness.

Listen carefully—"God is able to make every grace overflow to you, so that in every way, always having everything you need, you may excel in every good work" (2 Cor. 9:8). This law of sufficiency is not simply a law concerning *giving*; it is a law concerning *living*. It is impossible to live the Christian life in our own strength, but with God all things are possible.

Did you notice the repetition of the word "every" in this verse? "Every" translates the Greek word *pas*, which is often rendered *all*. Thus we have "all" grace . . . at "all" times . . . in "all" ways" . . . for "all" kinds of good deeds. The law of sufficiency, simply stated, is that when we have the heart to give or to serve, God will always make it possible for us to do so out of his own generosity (or *charis*).

Generous living might seem to be a risk to those who have little, but the risk disappears when we rely on the greatness of God's power. Our sufficiency does not come from our own ability, but it issues from the grace of God, which he desires to make overflow to us.

In one of my earlier pastorates, I was meeting with the budget committee, who asked me about my vision for the church. When I finished sharing my heart, the committee attempted to calculate the cost of funding such a vision. The cost greatly exceeded the amount they intended to raise the budget.

One individual asked me where I thought the money was coming from. I told the committee that my Father owned the cattle on a thousand hills and could easily sell a couple of head if needed.

They didn't seem to enjoy my weak attempt at humor. Then I shared with them my conviction that God was sufficient to meet our needs. I quoted one of my favorite verses: "Now to Him who is able to do above and beyond all that we ask or think—according to the power that works in you" (Eph. 3:20).

Many of us can quote the verse. The question is, can we live it?

The Law of Multiplication

Paul finally moved to a fourth law, which he introduced and supported by quoting from Psalm 112. The psalmist, in looking at the traits of the righteous, declared, "Happy is the man who fears the LORD, taking great delight in His commandments" (v. 1). In verse 3 he indicated that "wealth and riches are in his house, and his righteousness endures forever." This happy man lends generously and conducts his business fairly (v. 5).

But it is the first part of verse 9 to which Paul paid particular attention: "He distributes freely to the poor; his righteousness endures forever." "Righteousness" embraces all acts of piety, but in the context its most direct reference is almsgiving.

Paul, using words that sound almost like a benediction prayer, declared with clarity three things God has promised to do (2 Cor. 9:10). Paul employed future indicative verbs which give us an assurance that these promises are certain: (1) He will provide seed for the sower and bread for food; (2) he will multiply your seed; and (3) he will increase the harvest of your righteousness.

Paul declared God to be the universal provider, borrowing language from Isaiah 55:10, "seed to sow and food to eat." This is the foundational truth we learned in our study of Genesis. God is owner and provider, and we are his managers. Notice that the promise includes not only enough for our needs (our daily bread) but also additional resources for sowing or "giving."

As if this wasn't blessing enough, Paul declared that he would multiply the seed. When I read this promise, I am reminded of the story of Elisha and the multiplication of the widow's oil (2 Kings 4:2–6), as well as the story of Jesus multiplying the five loaves and two fish (Matt. 14). In Elisha's case every container was filled until no containers remained. In the narrative of the loaves and fish, the miracle was of such magnitude that "everyone ate and was filled. Then they picked up 12 baskets full of leftover pieces!" (Matt. 14:20).

God not only multiplies our seed for sowing, but he promises a fruitful harvest of righteousness. It is one thing to have sufficient seed; it is quite another to know that the seed sown will spring into life.

The language seems to recall the promise of Hosea 10:12: "Sow righteousness for yourselves and reap faithful love; break up your untilled ground. It is time to seek the LORD until He comes and sends righteousness on you like rain." God's purpose in providing and multiplying our seed is not to make us wealthy but to give us a fruitful ministry of righteousness.

What if the company you worked for gave you money to buy company stock? What if beyond that they gave you an additional share of stock for each share you purchased with the money they provided? And what if they guaranteed that the stock would always return a positive yield on the investment?

If that sounds too good to be true, just think of God's promise to supply what we need for effective ministry.

Can you imagine the impact we could have on our communities and the world if we took God's promises seriously? What would happen today in your own life if you dared to live, serve, and give knowing that God would supply and multiply the seed for sowing and would then provide a bountiful harvest? Would it impact your witnessing? Would it impact the time you commit to Bible study and ministry? Would it impact the resources you return to God for the reaching of the nations?

Too much is at stake for us not to take God at His word. We claim to believe the Bible is the inerrant Word of God, but are we willing to live by its promises?

The Results of Giving

For the ministry of this service is not only supplying the needs of the saints,
but is also overflowing in many acts of thanksgiving to God.

2 CORINTHIANS 9:12

Two girls gather grapes. One is happy for their taste and sweetness, but the other complains about the seeds.

Two women examine the same bush. One smells the roses, but the other can only see the thorns.

Two men hike a mountain. One enjoys the breathtaking view, but the other complains about the exertion it took to get there.

Two children sit down to dinner. One bows his head in gratitude, but the other complains about having to eat vegetables.

Have you ever found yourselves complaining about what others would consider to be a blessing? Most anyone with the resources to own this book has more to be thankful for than a large percentage of people who live in the world.

As the gospel songwriter Andraé Crouch asked, "How can I say thanks for the things You have done for me—Things so underserved, yet You give to prove Your love for me?" How do we express gratitude to God? As we will see today, one of the joyous outcomes of our giving is that it overflows in thanksgiving to God.

Giving Enriches Us

Isn't it just like God to allow our giving to become a reciprocal blessing to us? Our enrichment is certainly linked to our "harvest of . . . righteousness" (2 Cor. 9:10) that we looked at yesterday. Thus, as we grow in our giving, God gives us additional resources and additional opportunities to give.

We can certainly think of other ways our giving enriches us. We receive the joy of knowing that our giving supplies the needs of others (v. 12). Our giving enriches us in the building of our faith. It takes faith to give with the conviction that God will supply and multiply the seed, but when we act upon that faith, we actually grow in it.

Perhaps you read verse 11 closely enough to notice that even the enrichment is not for our benefit alone. We are enriched in every way "for all generosity." Life really isn't about us. We live to give glory and thanksgiving to God, and living with generosity provides us the opportunity to do just that.

Giving Meets Needs

Paul rejoiced in the clear assurance that the generous offering of the Corinthians would supply the needs of the saints in Jerusalem (v. 12). The phrase translated "for the ministry of this service" brings together two theologically charged words to describe the collection for Jerusalem. One is *diakonia*, which means "service," and the other is *leitergeo*, which means "ritual or cultic service." This latter word is used in Luke 1:23 to speak of Zachariah's service as a priest in the temple. In Hebrews 9:21 it is used in relationship with the vessels used in priestly service.

In other words, this offering was an act of worship on the part of the Corinthians that also meets the needs of the saints in Jerusalem.

Paul further articulated the theme of supplying the needs of the saints in 2 Corinthians 9:13 where he again underlined the generosity of the Corinthians "in sharing with them and with others." In verse 14 he indicated that the generosity of the Corinthians would have its reciprocal effect—that they would be enriched by the prayers of those to whom they ministered: "And in their prayers for you they will have a deep affection for you because of the surpassing grace of God on you."

This verse suggests that the generosity of the Corinthians would enlarge the circle of believers who would pray for them. What a bountiful return this would be for their generosity, as it is for ours! The verse may also suggest that the Jerusalem saints would long to see their benefactors and someday return the favor. Their affection for the Corinthians was based on the grace of God that the saints in Jerusalem saw manifested through the generous gift from people in Corinth they had never personally seen.

Generous living creates a wonderful cycle of blessing. Have you ever thought about those unnamed persons who may look you up in heaven someday because you gave to missions and enabled them to be saved? When you give to the poor, are you cognizant that you are ministering to Christ himself?

When you read this section in its entirety, you will notice that Paul alternated between the language of worship and that of practical ministry. Authentic worship will always lead to practical ministry just as doctrinal integrity should always produce right action.

Giving Inspires Gratitude

"Thanksgiving to God" dominated Paul's thoughts in this chapter. He repeated this emphasis three times in this short section (2 Cor. 9:11–12, 15). Thanksgiving is the attitude of heart that distinguishes the believer from the nonbeliever.

In Romans 1:21a, Paul noted, "For though they knew God, they did not glorify Him as God or show gratitude." Unbelievers do not comprehend that everything they have came from the hand of God. Therefore, they fail to respond with thanksgiving. Believers, on the other hand, "enter His presence with thanksgiving" (Ps. 95:2) and bring their requests before him "with thanksgiving" (Phil. 4:6).

In our present context it is the offering for the saints in Jerusalem that inspires expressions of thanksgiving. In 2 Corinthians 9:11, Paul noted that their generosity "produces thanksgiving to God through us." This verse is reminiscent of an earlier reference to thanksgiving found in 2 Corinthians 4:15, "For all this is because of you, so that grace, extended through more and more people, may cause thanksgiving to overflow to God's glory."

The context of that verse is instructive. Paul, perhaps speaking of himself and his coworkers, declared that they were but clay vessels into which God had poured his treasure to display his extraordinary power. Thus, it is resurrection power, embodied in the believer, that God uses to extend his grace "through more and more people," causing "thanksgiving to overflow to God's glory" (2 Cor. 4:15).

Returning to our present context now, we can see that it was the act of faith in sowing the seed—seed provided by God—that became the instrument through which God extended and demonstrated his grace to the saints in Jerusalem. This demonstration of grace caused the saints in Jerusalem to give thanks to God. Thus, it is most appropriate to state that their generosity was the trigger that produced this.

His language is even *more* effusive in 2 Corinthians 9:2, when he declared that their ministry not only supplied a need "but it is also overflowing in many acts of thanksgiving to God." The meaning of this is made clear in verse 13.

You might say there was a double dose of thanksgiving involved in all of this. First the Corinthians produced thanksgiving through their generosity, and then the recipients of that gift in turn thanked God, producing an overflow of thanksgiving to him.

Paul can't conclude this section without one final note of thanksgiving in verse 15. "Thanks be to God for His indescribable gift." The source or all grace and the model for all giving is God. The indescribable or inexpressible gift is the gift of God's Son. Paul offered a wonderful commentary on this in Romans 8:32, when he wrote, "He did not even spare His own Son, but offered Him up for us all; how will He not also with Him grant us everything?" You may recall that Paul had already appealed to the grace expressed by the Lord Jesus Christ who became poor through the offering of himself (2 Cor. 8:9) as the framework for Christian living and giving.

Have you ever thought that your ministry of giving is one avenue God gives you to produce overflowing thanksgiving to him? How it must please the heart of God when he sees his children trusting his Word, sowing his seed, and meeting the needs of others! When you write that check for your tithes and offerings—as you place it in the offering plate—listen by faith to hear the sound of thanksgiving crashing the gates of heaven.

Giving Glorifies God

If you thought the sound of thanksgiving was wonderful, Paul has yet another treat in store for you. "Through the proof of this service, they will glorify God for your obedience to the confession of the gospel of Christ" (v. 13a).

The sole end of man is to glorify God. And giving is one way to do it.

The language throughout this section indicates that Paul understood giving to be an appropriate act of worship for one who has received grace. The use of words like *leitergeo* and *eulogia* (which we have noted earlier) underlines this truth.

In Philippians 4:18, Paul thanked the members of that church for fully supplying his needs. He called their gift "a fragrant offering, a welcome sacrifice, pleasing to God." These are all terms of worship. We sometimes think of worship only in terms of the songs we sing and the confessions of faith we utter, but our giving is an act of worship that glorifies God. This offering not only demonstrated the obedience of the Corinthian believers and provided for the needs of others, but it also caused the saints in Jerusalem to glorify God.

Paul clearly anticipated that the offering, once received, would produce worship among the recipients, that they would glorify God both for the obedient confession of the gospel and for the generosity of sharing. Nothing shows more clearly the genuineness of our confession of the gospel than our willingness to give to meet the needs of others. In contrast, nothing reveals shallow commitment like covetousness and its companion stinginess.

Our giving has a theological significance that goes beyond the meeting of physical needs or subsidizing a church budget. It is an act of worship which pleases the Father.

I have encountered some people who like to give with great fanfare. You may recall the story of the widow and her small gift. The men preceding her gave with such ostentation that everyone noticed what they had given. The kingdom-focused person, however, gives so that all the glory and thanksgiving go to God, who provided the seed for sowing and even produces the harvest from the sowing.

Others want to give with strings attached so they can control where their money goes and how it is distributed. Has it dawned on you, though, that it was unlikely the Corinthian believers would ever see the saints in Jerusalem on this side of glory? Paul asked them to give generously and to trust Titus and the other brothers to care for the distribution of that gift. Kingdom people give in obedience, then trust God to provide the harvest.

Does your giving reflect adequately the grace you have received? Does it appropriately thank God for all he has done for you? Does it cause others to glorify and thank God for your generosity? Are you willing to give to reach and assist those you may never see?

Over 1.65 billion people alive today have little or no access to the gospel. Many wouldn't recognize the name *Jesus* if they could hear it spoken in their language. God's heartbeat is that every people group on the globe have the opportunity to worship him as rightful King. Does their spiritual hunger concern you? Does your giving to mission causes through your church reflect that concern?

Week 5, Day 5

A Strategy for Cooperative Giving

For Macedonia and Achaia were pleased to make a contribution
to the poor among the saints in Jerusalem.

ROMANS 15:26

We have all been awed by the force of a mighty river or held speechless by the vastness of a great lake. What we often fail to notice, though, are the hundreds of small streams that flow together, allowing the water flowing within their banks to join with that of others until all we see is the power of the river itself.

Paul actually envisioned an "overflow of grace" created as several churches allowed their offerings to run together to meet the needs of the saints at Jerusalem and to glorify the Father. This week we have gleaned several principles that should impact our personal giving, challenging us to joyously go beyond the tithe to generous giving, fully assured that God will provide the seed, multiply it, and assure the harvest. These promises are too good to ignore.

All the passages we have studied from the Corinthian letters this week deal with the collection for the poor in Jerusalem. Paul's priorities during the decade of the fifties was to rally the Gentile churches to a great task that would relieve the needs of those suffering and glorify God. Thus we can conclude that the Bible not only teaches individual stewardship but also corporate stewardship. We saw this in our study of the Old Testament as the tithes and offerings were brought to the Levites to be used in a corporate ministry.

Cooperative giving has certain unique characteristics: (1) It involves a task that is too large for any single church to accomplish on its own. (2) It allows all the churches to participate with equal sacrifice and joy, even though the size of the gifts may differ. (3) It both requires and builds unity among those participating. (4) It must be administrated with integrity and efficiency and distributed by those most capable of determining the needs. (5) It will enable the churches working together to meet the needs of the saints and glorify the Father.

Let's see that played out in the early New Testament church and imagine it working in ours.

Cooperative Giving Requires Mutual Concern

We can read about the offering being collected for the Jerusalem church in several different biblical locations—Romans 15:26; 2 Corinthians 8–9; Acts 11:27–30; 24:17. So there can be little doubt that this offering was an issue of great concern to the apostle Paul.

Simply stated, he was deeply concerned about the poor in Jerusalem. We don't know why this church was poorer than other churches. Jerusalem as a whole was not rich. Acts 11:28 mentions a famine that occurred during the reign of Claudius. But beyond this, it seems likely that the Jewish believers in Jerusalem had simply faced determined persecution from their neighbors and even from their family members. It is not far-fetched to suggest that many Jews, who dared to believe in Jesus as their Messiah, lost everything. We know that many of the members of the church in Jerusalem were scattered throughout the land of Judea by intense persecution (Acts 8).

A second motive behind Paul's passion for this offering was the fact that the Jews helped their poorer brethren as demanded by Old Testament law, just as the Greek religious brotherhoods cared for their own. Wouldn't it be a poor witness, then, if the Christians didn't demonstrate mutual concern for the poor in their own fellowship?

Further, when we read the book of Acts, we can discern that some of the Jewish brethren did not have a high regard for Paul's work among the Gentiles. He saw this offering as an opportunity to repay a debt to the Jewish brethren, to demonstrate the solidarity of the Gentile churches, and to bring unity between Jews and Gentiles (Rom. 15:27)—all of this at the same time.

Paul called upon all the churches in Achaia and Macedonia to work together because the need required an offering too large for any one church to meet. As we read 2 Corinthians 8, we find that Paul used the example of the Macedonians to encourage the believers in Corinth, just as he had used the eagerness of the churches in Achaia to encourage those in Macedonia. Further, because of his comment that the Macedonian churches had given out of great poverty (8:2), it is likely that he wanted the church at Corinth—who had greater resources to draw from—to desire to give with equal sacrifice.

The opportunity to give to a great cause beyond our local needs increases our vision and allows us to work together in a kingdom-sized venture.

Cooperative Giving Must Be Handled with Efficiency and Integrity

In 1 Corinthians 16:3, Paul indicated that the church at Corinth was to recommend by letter those whom they would like to deputize to convey the offering. He hoped that it would be possible for him to accompany the messengers on their journey to Jerusalem. And according to Acts 24:17, Paul was privileged to complete this task. "After many years, I came to bring charitable gifts and offerings to my nation."

In the second letter to the Corinthians we discover the criteria by which individuals were selected to administrate this large offering. The first name mentioned is Titus, who was a trustworthy friend of Paul's and of the church at Corinth. It is possible, in fact, that Titus was the bearer of the first letter to Corinth. He had certainly carried the painful letter referred to in 2 Corinthians—the one we don't have—and apparently had mediated the friendly relationship that existed between Paul and the Corinthians at the time this passage was written.

It is entirely possible that Titus had been involved in the gathering of the collection in Corinth.[4] We know at least that Paul indicated how God had put the same concern for the Corinthians in the heart of Titus as Paul himself felt (2 Cor. 8:16). We know that Titus's response to the invitation to administrate the collection was enthusiastic, "for he accepted our urging and, being very diligent, went out to you by his own choice" (8:17). Paul called Titus his partner and coworker in the service of the Corinthians (v. 23).

Paul also mentioned two other brothers who were to accompany Titus, but he didn't identify them other than by reference to their character. The first man mentioned is described as one "who is praised throughout the churches for his gospel ministry" (8:18). This brother was likely an evangelist or preacher of the gospel who was well-known and well-respected by several of the early churches.

The second unnamed brother had been tested in many circumstances on many different occasions and had been found to be diligent (8:22). Paul added that this man was excited about the forthcoming mission because of his great confidence in the Corinthians. Apparently, he had heard about their zeal to complete the offering.

Of the two unnamed brothers, it is sufficient to note that they were duly elected representatives of the churches and that they served for the glory of Christ (v. 23b).

Why did Paul take such careful precautions about the choice of those who would accompany the offering? Let's allow him to tell us in his own words. "We are taking this precaution so no one can find fault with us concerning this large sum administered by us. For we are making provision for what is honorable, not only before the Lord but also before men" (8:20–21).

In other words, Paul demanded that everything about this offering be above reproach. He was concerned not simply for his reputation before *men* but knew that he was even more so accountable to God.

Church members and church staff alike are responsible to God and accountable before men to handle God's money honestly and efficiently. The church should select diligent men who will employ efficient methods, who will stand accountable to others and to God in the administration of the funds collected for ministry. One of the reasons Billy Graham's ministry has stood the test of time when so many others have fallen by the wayside is because of the high level of integrity that has been demonstrated in reporting and handling the resources provided to that organization for ministry.

Cooperative Giving Must Have a Kingdom Focus

Fortunately for our study, Paul gave us several clear indications of the motivation behind this offering. Thus, we might look at four characteristics of corporate giving that indicate it has kingdom focus.

1. *Kingdom giving supplies the needs of the saints.* This is such a consistent theme of this section, we could almost put our finger down on any one of several verses and find this emphasis. In 2 Corinthians 8:4, Paul indicated

that the Macedonians begged for the privilege of sharing in the ministry to the saints. In 2 Corinthians 9:11, he encouraged the Corinthians to complete the offering because it supplied the needs of the saints.

Paul referred to this grand offering as "fellowship," "service," "grace," "blessing," and "divine service." Every Christian belongs to a bigger community, and therefore we cannot live the Christian life in isolation. The needs of the saints are our needs, as well. When one member of the body suffers, we all suffer together (1 Cor. 12:25–26). Giving to meet the needs of others provides a cure for our spiritual "my-opia"—the dread disease that causes Christians to focus only on their own needs and desires.

2. *Kingdom giving indicates the genuineness of our love.* In 2 Corinthians 8:8, Paul indicated that he would not "command" them to give to this offering because "I am testing the genuineness of your love." Later in the same passage he challenged the Corinthians, "Therefore, before the churches, show them the proof of your love and of our boasting about you" (8:24). In Romans 15:27 he mentioned that the Gentiles were indebted to the Jews since they had shared in their spiritual benefits.

The gospel had originated among the Jews and had come to them through Jewish Christian missionaries, himself among them. There can be little question that Paul saw this offering as an opportunity for the Gentile churches to gain credibility, proving that they had received grace.

And certainly all of us owe a debt to grace. That debt is not only to God but to others who have gone before us in the faith. None of us come to Christ in a vacuum. Thus, it is critical that we exercise good stewardship to demonstrate the genuineness of our love. If there is any one arena that reveals weak faith, it is the area of Christian stewardship. Those afraid to give indicate they do not trust God to provide and multiply the seed. Further, kingdom giving requires us to give with no strings attached to people we may not see, and perhaps never will see. Kingdom giving requires that we give to causes so large that we can't get individual credit for what we have given.

3. *Kingdom giving expands the reach of the gospel.* Is it possible that one of the reasons Paul was so passionate about this offering for the saints in Jerusalem was his concern that his brethren in the flesh come to know Christ? Paul testified to his heart's desire in Romans 10:1: "Brothers, my heart's desire and prayer to God concerning them is for their salvation." Later in Romans 11 he indicated why he magnified his ministry to the Gentiles. "Now I am speaking to you Gentiles. In view of the fact that I am an apostle to the Gentiles, I magnify my ministry, if I can somehow make my own people jealous and save some of them" (Rom. 11:13–14). The generous offering by the Gentiles to the Jewish believers in Jerusalem would be an

undeniable testimony to the non-Christian Jews living in Jerusalem, perhaps motivating them to receive the gospel.

All kingdom giving is motivated by the desire to see God's kingdom advanced. For that reason it is critical, at both the individual and corporate level, that we give in such a manner that it advances God's kingdom.

Too many believers want to give to their pet projects without due concern for the kingdom. Others want credit for their giving and thus are unwilling to give where they can't see or control it. Kingdom givers have no concern for control or credit. Their one concern is for God's kingdom and his glory.

4. *Kingdom giving glorifies the Father.* In the section where Paul gave directions for the administration of the offering (2 Cor. 8:16–24), he twice mentioned the ultimate goal that kingdom giving gives glory to God. He spoke of the gift "that is being administered by us for the glory of the Lord Himself" (v. 19). When he described the messengers who would be responsible for getting it safely and in its entirety to the believers in Jerusalem, he indicated that they were "the messengers of the churches, the glory of Christ" (8:23).

The ultimate goal of man is to glorify God. Therefore, all of our living and giving should be directed toward that end. Paul had already told them: "Whether you eat of drink, or whatever you do, do everything for God's glory" (1 Cor. 10:31).

A quick glance at Scripture indicates that God is to be glorified in our worship (Ps. 50:23), in our good works (Matt. 5:16), in our fruitful living (John 15:8), in our spiritual unity (Rom. 15:6), and in the use of our bodies (1 Cor. 6:20). John 17 provides an instructive lesson on glory. The Son declares that his mission had been to glorify the Father and reveal his name (vv. 1–6). If you know that passage well, you will recall that Jesus prayed for his disciples and for the ones who would believe through their witness. The purpose of his prayer? "I have given them the glory You have given me" (John 17:22a).

Our giving provides us with the opportunity to glorify the Father. That's why individuals and churches who give in order to receive the credit for their giving rob God of the glory that is rightfully his. The kingdom-focused giver's singular concern is to give in such a manner that it *embodies his name, advances his kingdom,* and *accomplishes his will.*

Practical Implications

Just as individuals have a personal accountability for stewardship, local congregations have a corporate responsibility. Churches must ensure that resources are managed with integrity and efficiency. And they must plan their giving with several objectives in mind:

1. *Every church should make sure their budget reflects God's heartbeat for the nations.* You should look to see how the resources are allocated related to Jerusalem, Judea, Samaria, and the ends of the earth. While a significant amount may be allocated to Jerusalem (the local community), a sufficient and generous amount must be included for the other three quadrants of responsibility—your state, the nation, and the world.

2. *The church budget should not be based on what is presently being received or what is required "to keep the doors open."* It must be based on the command and resources of the risen Lord. The church must invade the world with the gospel.

3. *The church must exercise faith if it expects its membership to exercise faith.* The budget cannot be based solely on the size of the congregation without due consideration to the size of our God. We have a big God who has given us a big command, and he expects us to complete it. Most believers and most churches are underchallenged and undermotivated.

4. *In developing a budget, mission must determine ministry.* Ministry is translated into dollars via the budget. Motivation for giving must be the glory of God and the reaching of the nations.

5. *Don't let geographical distance dim your vision.* We can more readily see local needs, and they often have vocal proponents, but our budget concerns must be dictated by the heart of God.

6. *Every church must work together with other like-minded churches to fulfill the Great Commission,* invading the four quadrants of concern indicated by the Acts 1:8 challenge. No single church can sufficiently reach any one of the four quadrants. We must not only find like-minded churches to partner with, but we must reflect these partnerships in our budgeting process.

Most denominations provide avenues for churches to work together for the spread of the gospel beyond Jerusalem, beyond our local communities. And the kingdom-focused church will share in these endeavors without worrying about getting credit for it.

Startling Facts

I close out this week's readings by looking forward to the final section of the book where we'll discuss in challenging but specific terms the ways churches like yours can cooperate with others to achieve kingdom goals. But in preparation for that, let's look at a few telling statistics—numbers that paint an interesting picture of where we are today—that help us imagine what it may require to go where God is leading us to go together.

• The average church member gave 2.5 percent of their income through the local church in 1992.[5]

• All research shows that a minority of members give most of the money. As a rule of thumb, 75 percent of the money in the typical church is given by 25 percent of the people.[6]

• Since the 1950s, Protestant churches have spent increasing proportions of their money on local operations and programs and decreasing proportions on missions and denominational causes. In the mid-1990s, an average of 10 to 15 percent of all contributions were being spent on missions outside the church, whereas in the 1950s, the figure was roughly twice as high.[7]

• Income for overseas mission expenditures through more than six hundred agencies, including denominational, interdenominational, and independent agencies, was $2.9 billion in 2002. How does this compare with our spending in other areas? Domestic box office receipts topped $9 billion in 2002. In 1998, $23 billion was spent in pet-related stores. In 2001, Americans spent $38 billion on state lotteries.[8]

Staggering insights indeed. What will we do with them?

Compounding Interest and Kingdom Cooperation

Week 6, Day 1

First and Last Words

But you will receive power when the Holy Spirit has come upon you,
and you will be My witnesses in Jerusalem, in all Judea
and Samaria, and to the ends of the earth.

ACTS 1:8

Certain words are so memorable than we treasure them forever. New parents or grandparents wait with anticipation to record baby's first words. We secretly hope they might say our name first, especially after we've privately coached them to say "dada" or "mama." More often than not, though, it is something generic like "ball." But no matter, we duly record it in our baby book.

Last words, however, may actually have a more lasting impact. I've watched families gather around a bedside straining to hear the last words of a loved one. My sister recounts a moving story of some of my dad's final words. Dad had not communicated verbally for several days. It was a Sunday morning, and Dot was trying to coax him to respond by telling him what day it was and that he needed to get ready for church.

Somehow the message penetrated the deep fog of his near comatose condition, and he rallied long enough to whisper the refrain from a much-loved hymn: "For all my sins my Savior went to Calvary." Our family has cherished that story and those words that were an appropriate ending for my dad.

I find it fascinating that Jesus' first sermon focused on God's kingdom (Matt. 4:17) and his last words (Matt. 28:19–20; Acts 1:3–8) focused on that same kingdom. Many preachers have done sermon series based on the last words uttered on the cross—and those are certainly moving and powerful words—but they weren't Jesus' last words. His last words to his followers were uttered in his resurrected body.

The kingdom. First and last. And everything in between. That was Jesus' message to the people of his day. It remains his heartbeat to us even now.

The Great Commission

Matthew, Mark, and Luke are called the Synoptic Gospels, in part because they follow the life of Christ in a similar and sequential fashion. Thus, it is not surprising that they each end with a command we have called "The Great Commission."

We generally quote the Great Commission from Matthew's Gospel. "All authority has been given to Me in heaven and on earth. Go, therefore, and make disciples of all nations, baptizing them in the name of the Father and of the Son and of the Holy Spirit, teaching them to observe everything I have commanded you. And remember, I am with you always, to the end of the age" (28:18–20).

The Gospel writers were transparent about the reaction of the early disciples to the appearance of the resurrected Lord. Matthew tells us that when they saw him they worshipped, but with total honesty he adds "but some doubted" (28:17). Mark tells us further that Jesus rebuked their unbelief and hardness of heart (Mark 16:14). Thus, we see worship, fear, and unbelief colliding in the hearts of the early believers.

So on the surface it didn't look like an auspicious beginning for the church of the resurrected Lord—those whom he had said would have possession of the "keys of the kingdom" and against whose witness the "forces of Hades" would flee in retreat (Matt. 16:13–19). But that is precisely who they were, and that is exactly what will occur.

I'm afraid we have read this passage so often, however, that we fail to fully comprehend its radical nature. We sometimes fail to remember that these words of Christ are an imperative. They are a *command*, not a *suggestion*.

The mandate to these early followers of Jesus was that they were to disciple all nations. They were to accomplish this task in the natural activities of every day—being God's "movable possession," expanding his kingdom everywhere they went. The "baptizing" and "teaching" component of the mandate suggested a comprehensive plan for accomplishing the task.

If this seems like a daunting assignment, tighten your seat belt, because it gets bigger. They were to do this in the context of "all nations."

This term *nations* occurs 164 times in the Bible and can be translated "race," "nation," or "people group." Can you hear again God's heartbeat as it permeates the pages of Scripture? God has an agenda, and that agenda involves "all nations." He is their rightful King, and he wants every people group on Earth to have the opportunity to worship him as King.

Does this sound like an impossible task for a small group of frightened, sometimes doubtful believers? It was.

But Matthew included some incredible news that gave them reason for confidence. This universal mission was to be accomplished with universal authority. Jesus declared, "All authority has been given to Me in heaven and on earth."

Matthew's Gospel focuses throughout on Jesus' authority. The disciples had most likely witnessed it every day in his teaching ministry (Matt. 7:29), in his healing of disease (8:1–13), and in his ability to declare sin forgiven (9:6). But the distinctive word here is *"all."* As the resurrected Savior, Jesus' authority was now complete and comprehensive. He had defeated all enemies. He was totally without rival.

The significance of his authority for the early church was made clear in his last statement—"I am with you always, to the end of the age." The Lord who has *all authority* promised to be with them *always*. Thus, they would never approach their task with limited power but with total power.

And neither do we. God has all the resources necessary to accomplish the task of global evangelism. Do you believe that he will give us today the resources to finish the task?

Luke recorded the same global commission but with a slightly different emphasis. He recounted several actions of Jesus that were intended to assist the disciples as they struggled to believe.

Jesus showed them his hands and feet and invited them to touch him. Then he asked for food and ate it in their presence (24:39–43). He reminded them of his earthly teaching and opened their minds so they could understand how the Old Testament Scriptures had pointed to this moment of fulfillment—how the suffering, death, and resurrection of the Messiah had all been foretold.

So now this good news was to be proclaimed in his name to all nations, beginning in Jerusalem. The final words of Jesus in Luke's account (24:49) are somewhat different from those in Matthew, but the impact is the same. "And look, I am sending you what My Father promised. As for you, stay in the city until you are empowered from on high."

All they needed had been given—and would continue to be given—by the power of the promised Holy Spirit.

The Empowering Spirit

Luke's Gospel is actually written in two parts. The book we call Luke is the first part, and the book of Acts is the second. In Acts 1:1, Luke reminded us how in his first narrative he included all that Jesus did and taught right up to the moment that he gave the "orders" or "commission" to his chosen disciples and was taken up from the earth. Verse 3 then gives us a summary statement of those final events. "After He had suffered, He also presented Himself alive to them by many convincing proofs, appearing to them during 40 days and speaking about the kingdom of God."

The term "convincing proofs" literally means "infallible proofs"— evidence of such a clarion nature that no doubt could remain in the hearts and minds of the disciples concerning the fact that Jesus had been bodily raised from the dead. Faith in the resurrection was important because their power was dependent on it. Further, the message they were to declare was based on it (Rom. 10:9–10; 1 Cor. 15:1–8).

But we are not told a great deal about the forty days of postresurrection appearances. Notice, however, that we are told about the content of his teaching. And what was Jesus primarily talking about?

The kingdom of God.

Jesus had a singular focus. During his earthly ministry, he focused on his Father's kingdom. So why would we expect him to do any different after his resurrection?

These final messages were critical, though, because the kingdom would no longer be *among them* in the presence of Christ (Luke 17:21); it would be *in them* through the presence of the Holy Spirit. The kingdom message would now be *their* message. The kingdom cause had now become *their* cause. The expansion of the kingdom to the ends of the earth would be accomplished through them—*and through us!*

Tragically some of his early disciples were still focused on a future political kingdom (Acts 1:6) that might exalt them to levels of influence.

Jesus did not rebuke them, but he clearly refocused them. The kingdom was not about Israel or about them; it was about the Father.

But as we mentioned earlier, Jesus told them to wait first for the Father's promise (Acts 1:4; Luke 24:49)—the Holy Spirit. John the Baptist had announced this spiritual empowering (Matt. 3:11; Mark 1:8; Luke 3:16). And once the waiting period was over, Jesus said they would be able to accomplish more in terms of the kingdom than even he had accomplished in his limited time of earthly ministry (John 14:16–18, 26; 15:26–27; 16:7–15).

The power and resources for kingdom advance came from the Holy Spirit, not from any human source. And still today the kingdom advances only as the Holy Spirit accomplishes extraordinary things through ordinary people.

When the Holy Spirit came upon the first disciples, they became his witnesses. The word *witness* is a key word in the book of Acts, occurring twenty-nine times in either a verb or noun form. The English word *martyr* also comes from the Greek word we translate *witness*. Those who have received the Spirit would lay their lives down for the gospel.

And though the means of kingdom advance may sound simple—Holy Spirit-empowered believers telling what God has done in their lives—it still remains the force that turns the world upside down. Sometimes we can get so sophisticated and make things so complicated that we forget the simplicity of God's plan for kingdom advance. But nothing has changed! God will expand his kingdom through us as we bear witness by the power of the Holy Spirit.

The Strategy of Expansion

Jesus had told his followers that kingdom explosion would begin in Jerusalem and expand exponentially from there to Judea and Samaria until the ends of the earth had been encompassed in the kingdom. A quick glance at the book of Acts helps us see that this verse serves as an outline of the book.

Acts 1–7 speaks of Jerusalem, Acts 8–9 encompasses Judea and Samaria, and the remainder of the book focuses on the ends of the earth. The word translated *ends* or *uttermost* means the "lowest," "extreme," "last in temporal succession," "to the end." God intends that his kingdom be advanced to the most extreme parts of the earth. *Nowhere* and *no people* are to remain outside his reign.

When we read the book of Acts, we discover a clear strategy of expansion. The early disciples shared their witness, and hearers were regularly converted, baptized, and added to the fellowship of believers (Acts 2:41). All of this was accomplished in the context of the early church's everyday activity: "They devoted themselves to the apostle's teaching, to fellowship, to the breaking of bread, and to prayers" (v. 42).

The level of their fellowship and physical concern for one another exceeds anything most of us have ever known. They sold possessions and property and distributed the proceeds to all whenever anyone had a need (2:45). My mentor, Mark Corts, used to refer to the early church as a "no-need church." Whenever they discovered a need, they pooled their resources to meet that need and advance the kingdom.

The description of this church in Scripture is so moving, in fact, it seems best just to let the Bible speak without commentary. "Every day they devoted themselves to meeting together in the temple complex, and broke bread from house to house. They ate their food with gladness and simplicity of heart, praising God and having favor with all the people. And every day the Lord added to them those who were being saved" (2:46–47).

Wow! Wouldn't you love to belong to a fellowship like that? There is no reason we can't! Our churches could well exhibit the same characteristics today because the strategy for kingdom advance and the empowering by the Spirit remain the same. Don't they? God continues to advance his kingdom as churches grow and plant other healthy growing churches, extending the boundaries, stretching the limits.

We must never forget that God created the world with sufficient resources to accomplish the task of advancing his kingdom to the ends of the earth. He is still looking for a people who will use his resources by his plans and for his purpose. Will you be that person, and will your church be that church?

Will you use the material provisions he has placed within your grasp to fulfill his Great Commission?

Going Forward

In order to do so, we need to remember a few important principles:
- *Everything begins with the local church.* The Acts 1:8 covenant was not given to a denomination or a para-church ministry. It was given to the church.
- *Each church must have a strategic plan for each quadrant*—Jerusalem, Judea, Samaria, and the ends of the earth—the city, the state, the nation, and the world.

- *The Holy Spirit remains our sole source of supply.* His empowerment is the only thing that can enable us to use his resources well in accomplishing kingdom advance.
- *His resources are wide and varied.* They include both our Spirit-empowered witness and the material resources sufficient for reaching the nations.

And don't forget this—*no single church can fulfill even a part of the Acts 1:8 covenant* without developing partnerships with other like-minded churches. If we are to take this kingdom mandate seriously, it will involve joining with our brothers and sisters in Christ to pursue this challenge together.

In the next section we will look at a group of churches who have made an attempt to develop a cooperative strategy for reaching the nations that includes both strategic mission initiatives and the resources to fund those initiatives.

I pray that your church will see the potential and necessity of this.

Week 6, Day 2

A Living Model of Cooperative Missions

Go, therefore, and make disciples of all the nations, baptizing them in the name of the Father and the Son and the Holy Spirit.

MATTHEW 28:19

The old question of how to eat an elephant still has the same answer: One bite at a time! But truly, the task of discipling the world seems so elephantine that it is convenient just to ignore it.

If you've traveled abroad, you've been made even more aware of the immensity of the task. My wife, Paula, recently went to India with a group of women and was staggered by the vast numbers of people there who still need to hear about Christ's love. They are not lost because they've rejected the gospel; they have simply never had the opportunity to hear it! There is one paid minister for every eight million people in India. If we experienced that same ratio in America, it would mean that we had only thirty-seven paid Christian workers for our entire nation!

It would be so easy to allow such statistics to paralyze us into inactivity if it weren't for the fact that discipling the nations is a command of God, not a suggestion.

It would be easy to see it as an impossible task if it weren't for the promise of the risen Lord that he would be with us as we go.

Thus, we are assured that the resources are available for us to complete this task before the King returns. And as we have already acknowledged, the local church is the centerpiece of God's strategy to advance his kingdom.

But if local churches are going to complete this task, they must be intentional, globally focused, and cooperative. The task demands that each church form partnerships with like-minded churches for the sake of the kingdom.

Cooperation is key!

But what goes into these kinds of partnerships? First, cooperation is *voluntary*. Second, it demands a *shared vision*. Third, it is based on *mutual trust* that emerges from *shared convictions*. Finally, it requires *kingdom thinking*. The kingdom-focused church is not concerned about getting any credit; it is only concerned about the most effective and efficient method for completing the task.

So I want us to look in this chapter at a living model that many missiologists view as one of the most effective strategies ever devised for allowing local churches to work together to accomplish the Acts 1:8 mandate. The Southern Baptist Convention is made up of 42,465 churches ranging from small family churches to well-known megachurches that have chosen to cooperate with one another for the advancement of the kingdom.

And it works. Here's how it all came about.

Early Associations

It didn't take long for individual Baptist churches to realize that both their ministry and their fellowship were enhanced by banding together in local associations. We don't know the exact date of the earliest association, but we know that English Separatists and Baptists viewed associations as autonomous organizations that served in an advisory role to the local church.

In America the first association of Baptist churches was formed in Philadelphia in 1707. We also know that later on, in 1775, the Sandy Creek Baptist Church became the first Separate Baptist Church in North Carolina, and within three years nine Baptist churches had formed the Sandy Creek Baptist Association. These autonomous churches treasured their independence, but they also began to recognize their interdependence. They realized the task before them was so immense that they must band together for effective ministry.[1]

Two Trains of Thought

In 1814 a wider avenue of cooperative mission was initiated to assist the local church in its call to go to the ends of the earth. The General Missionary Convention (also known as the Triennial Convention) was developed to provide support for missionaries like Adoniram Judson. While the term *convention* was used at this stage, it actually functioned more like a society in terms of funding.

Two methods for funding cooperative mission ministry were used in America, even before the Triennial Convention. In 1776 the Philadelphia Association established a *permanent missionary fund*, "the interest whereof to be by them laid out every year in support of ministers traveling on the errand of the churches, or otherwise, as the necessities of said churches shall require."[2] This fund was gathered in quarterly collections and administered by the association. Soon other associations had followed suit.

Then in 1802 the Shaftesbury Association in Vermont actually appointed a committee to handle mission contributions, examine candidates, consider time and place of appointment, and administer salaries.[3] Here we can see the seeds of the pattern of mission funding and administration that has become synonymous with the Southern Baptist Convention.

A second method of funding was also being used by some Baptist churches and associations. It was called the *societal method*, modeled after the mission work of William Carey and others through the Baptist Missionary Society of England. The societal method essentially was a method for funding each unique mission with little coordination or administration. Simply stated, a society was an independent organization of loosely connected individuals who desired to support a specific cause.

During the first several decades of the 1800s, Baptist churches in America were confronted with the dilemma of determining whether they would adopt the societal method of supporting missions or a more denominational approach like that adopted by the Philadelphia Association. Southerner Richard Furman clearly favored the denominational, associational approach, recommending a "general denominational body to promote ministerial education and domestic missions in addition to foreign missions."[4] When the Triennial Convention formed in 1814, it appeared that the convention would move in this direction.

But key Northern leaders argued against centralized denominational structure and moved the convention back to a system in which each benevolent ministry was completely autonomous, thus favoring a societal method of funding. This became one of the tensions that ultimately led to the division between Baptists in the North and South.

The churches and leaders of the South didn't like the societal method for missions because it lacked focus and wasn't an efficient way for carrying out the Great Commission. They began to observe, in a period beginning in 1802 and lasting a little over a hundred years, that eleven different foreign mission societies had been established along with twenty-two more conducted by women's groups.

These societies were essentially unrelated, with goals and ministries that frequently overlapped. Yet because the representative of a particular society was more committed to the cause of his or her group than to any overarching strategy, these entities continued to function, duplicating efforts and covering largely the same ground. This meant the local church was virtually under siege by fund-raisers from the various societies. This model was neither efficient nor kingdom focused.

Starting and Stopping

A decisive kingdom moment occurred on May 8, 1845.

In Augusta, Georgia, 293 delegates from various Baptist entities in the South met to determine whether they ought to form an entity separate from the Triennial Convention. William Bullein Johnson of South Carolina came to the convention with a draft for a new constitution that featured both foreign and home mission societies under one governing organization. "Thus in contrast to the Triennial structure with separate, autonomous, and independent societies for each benevolence, the Southern Baptist Convention provided for one body that would promote all benevolences that commended themselves to it, with an emphasis on denominational unity rather than any single benevolence."[5]

This radical departure from the societal method placed cooperation and kingdom above individual agendas. The overarching issues became efficiency and effectiveness.

This new convention was to have separate and distinct boards for each ministry, located at different places but each accountable to the Convention. The first official convention of the newly formed body met in Richmond, Virginia, in 1846. It was made up of 4,126 churches, 351,951 members, and recorded 23,222 baptisms that first year.[6]

The mission focus was clearly in view as J. B. Jeter was chosen to head the Foreign Mission Board and Basil Manly was selected for the Domestic Mission Board. The issue of funding, however, was still on the table.

At the end of the session of the first Southern Baptist Convention meeting, one offering was taken for foreign missions and another for domestic missions. Soon these organizations employed agents to promote their mission cause and to solicit funds, allowing agents to keep about 20 percent of what they collected. By the time expenses were added in, however, it meant that 25 percent of the money raised was consumed in the process of raising money.[7]

So not only was this an expensive method of fund-raising, but small churches were sometimes neglected by the mission agents while larger churches were overwhelmed by their openhanded visits. Fund-raising rallies and appeals at associational meetings only added to the clamor for more funds.

The bold attempt to organize churches for cooperative missions was hindered by a mixing of associational organization with societal funding, which was woefully ineffective in the raising of sufficient funds to make a global impact and was inefficient in terms of the high cost of fund-raising. Thus for seventy-five years the vision of Johnson and others was hindered by the lack of a cooperative funding mechanism.

But Southern Baptists soon began their search for a more effective way to carry on cooperative, kingdom work.

A Kingdom-Focused Decision

In 1908 the convention appointed an Apportionment Committee for setting state goals for church contributions to home and foreign missions. Then in 1913 the convention began to study the structure and plans of its organization to see whether they were effective "for soliciting, combining, and directing the energies of Southern Baptists and for securing the highest efficiency of our forces and the fullest possible enlistment of our people for the work of the Kingdom."[8] Even at this early stage the focus was on efficiency for the sake of the kingdom.

But the expanding denomination was experiencing growing pains. The Convention was a large but loose-knit group of churches, committed to a collective vision based on the Great Commission but with minimal overarching strategy or structure. So in 1917 the Executive Committee was established to bring structure and improve efficiency to a rapidly growing denomination. As history shows, this was a timely and critical decision.

On the opening morning of the 1919 Convention, President J. B. Gambrell called for the adoption of an enlarged program that would call Southern Baptist people to a demonstration of the value of orthodoxy in free action. In response a committee on the Financial Aspect of the Enlarged Program recommended that the Convention raise seventy-five million dollars during the next five years. The Campaign Committee, headed by First Baptist Dallas pastor, George Truett, was appointed. L. R. Scarborough, president of Southwestern Seminary, became general director of the campaign and, with the permission of the seminary trustees, took time away from the seminary to assist in this bold fund-raising campaign.

The campaign was aggressively promoted throughout 1919, and more than 92.5 million dollars was pledged. People from all arenas of life met to pray for the campaign, committing to do their part. By the time of the 1920 Convention, more than twelve million dollars from the original pledges had been given. But tragically, the depression hit hard at the end of the five-year campaign, and Scarborough had to report to the Convention that only 58.5 million had been raised, far short of original hopes and projections.

Many viewed the shortfall only in terms of failure. But in retrospect the seventy-five million-dollar campaign may be one of the "grandest failures" of all times because the amount raised during the Great Depression was more than the total of all gifts given to the denomination in the previous seventy-four years combined! Around nine thousand churches that had not previously committed *anything* to denominational causes pledged and gave to this new cooperative effort. Further, Catherine Allen notes that the campaign introduced a trio of mind-sets that revolutionized Southern Baptist life—a prototype for the Cooperative Program, a unified church budget, and an every-member canvass for giving.[9]

The 1924 Southern Baptist Convention meeting in Atlanta called for the churches to complete the seventy-five million campaign and to conduct an every-member canvass of individual pledges for state and convention-wide causes. This canvass would assist the states and the national convention in forming their budgets. An organizational strategy that included state and national work was clearly emerging.

In 1923 M. E. Dodd was appointed chairman of the Committee of Future Program, which was commissioned with the task of putting the denominational work on a substantial, permanent, and continuous basis. Dodd and other convention leaders saw this program not simply as a response to financial issues raised by the failure to reach the seventy-five million-dollar goal but as a long-term answer to mission needs. "Not only is the New Program a kingdom necessity, it is also our Program. We made it. It is the result of the best thinking of our denomination, led as we believe by the Spirit of God. It is Scriptural."[10]

The Cooperative Program was visionary yet simple. Local churches were to canvass members for committed giving through the local church to a unified budget. Churches would then set their annual budgets, committing a percentage of their total revenue to the Cooperative Program. That percentage gift would be sent to the state convention, hopefully on a monthly basis. The state convention would then maintain a percentage of those gifts for its own mission ministry, and the remainder was to be sent to the national convention for worldwide causes. The original goal was for the state and the national convention to split these receipts fifty-fifty. The SBC would then set its own budget based on anticipated receipts.

This new method was radical, to be sure, but had much to commend it. "The Future Program Committee contended that the new approach was simple, permanent, responsible, unifying, ambitious, thoughtful, cooperative, visionary, biblical and God honoring."[11] The convention would face new challenges related to cooperative giving in the years to come, and nuanced changes were required to the Cooperative Program strategy, but this simple kingdom-focused strategy would become one of the most effective and efficient tools ever devised to fulfill the Acts 1:8 challenge in a cooperative, kingdom-focused manner.

Clearly, what stands out in this short historical sketch was the desire to be efficient, effective, and kingdom focused in the use of missions funding—issues that remain relevant and desirable for churches and individuals today. Will we use God's resources with kingdom focus? Will we find the most efficient and effective manner for reaching the ends of the earth without concern for control or glory?

Will we cooperate to do more together than any one of us can do alone? What will happen if we don't?

Week 6, Day 3

The Mutual Fund of Missions

On the first day of the week, each of you is to set something aside
and save to the extent that he prospers, so that no collections
will need to be made when I come.

1 Corinthians 16:2

How would you like to have someone like John Templeton or Peter Lynch investing your money? Pretty simple question, isn't it, when you take into consideration that these two men have become synonymous with successful investing. If they would just take the little bit of money we own and put it together with all the millions they have invested, we could profit substantially from their knowledge and expertise.

But as we have noted, Americans tend to save at low levels. Why do you think that's the case?

I'm sure our first excuse is that we don't have enough money above expenses to worry about saving and investing. When I was at Southwestern Seminary, though, I loved to tell the story of the lady I read about who took in washing for a living, yet who not only provided for her own children's needs but also saved a large amount of additional money to fund scholarships for poor children. Truth is, if your motivation is sufficiently high, you will find the resources to invest. But first, you must make a commitment to do it!

The second barrier for many people comes from the practical question of *how* to invest. If you think you have a lot of options when you reach for the remote control to change the channel on your TV set, just pick up your paper, open to the financial page, and prepare yourself for investor's paralysis. Stocks, bonds, mutual funds, certificates of deposit, precious metals, savings accounts—these are just a small sampling of the plethora of opportunities open to the average investor.

But truly, that's just the tip of the iceberg. Once you dive in and make a commitment to invest, some well-meaning friend will come along and tell you about the importance of keeping a balance between large caps, mid caps, and small caps. If you're hardy enough to survive the advice of these friends who know precisely what you should do, the fees for buying stocks and other investment products can cool your ardor in a hurry.

It's just too much information. The average investor simply doesn't have the resources, the expertise, or the time to make wise decisions about all these options, and thus many of us sit on the sidelines and watch the Dow go up without us. Panic sets in as we think we are the only ones missing out on the big rally. Then along comes a friend with a "surefire," "can't-miss," inside tip on a stock that's ripe for a double or even a triple return. So you plop down your hard-earned cash only to see this stock go "belly up," and you're back to the sidelines.

In recent years mutual-fund companies have attempted to solve the dilemma of the small investor by employing a team of experts who will select and manage our portfolio for us. Some mutual funds are designed with the intent of mirroring a balanced portfolio. So the solution for many small and large investors is to buy a well-balanced mutual fund that is *managed by a trusted advisor who has a proven track record.* Such a strategy minimizes risk and maximizes return.

It makes one think of another trusted Advisor who has an even more sterling history of performance and who can promise a return on our investment that is a lot more valuable than money.

Kingdom Investing

My real interest in this section, of course, is about investing in the kingdom on both the individual and the corporate level. In many ways, though, we face some of the same investing dilemmas we've just talked about when it comes to kingdom investing. For example:

How can the small amount of my tithes and offerings make a difference for the kingdom of God? How can our church really impact Jerusalem,

Judea, Samaria, and the ends of the earth? What's the best way to ensure that our money is maximized and used well in authentic missions endeavors? How do we know which places to invest our support with so many worthy options to choose from? And how do we still maintain the proper level of at-home funding to keep our bills paid and our members served?

These are serious questions to ask because the King is serious about getting his resources in the hands of people who will join him in reaching the nations. Some people and some churches have hidden behind the excuse that their small amount can't make a kingdom-sized impact. How else do we explain data that shows how giving by American church members declined steadily between 1968 and 1998 from 2.45 percent to 2.12 percent?[12] If the tithe is the place of beginning, and if God desires his people to move forward to generous, spontaneous, grace giving, the King must be grieved by our failure to invest his resources in his kingdom.

Still other people and churches have been paralyzed in their kingdom investing because they don't know where they can find that balanced mutual fund with a trusted advisor with a proven track record. I suppose every Christian has sat in a church meeting and heard an appeal for a mission need that sounded like an investment that was "too good to miss." So we responded. But later we were disappointed to find that the money was wasted because there was little strategy and no accountability. This kind of experience has prompted some kingdom investors to head for the sidelines.

But that's not really an option when missiologists estimate that 1.65 billion people today have little or no access to the gospel! Thus we must find a trusted advisor, a balanced mutual fund of missions, and pool our resources with hundreds and thousands of other believers who share our convictions and have the King's heartbeat.

Yesterday we began our look at the Southern Baptist Convention's attempt at developing a mutual fund of missions. Let's look further to see if it meets our criteria for good kingdom investing.

How the Cooperative Program Works

The simplicity of the Cooperative Program is one of the reasons this was chosen as an example of kingdom investing. Everything begins where it should—and where it must—with the local church. Let's watch how this progression takes shape.

1. *The local church.* Every church should have a unified budget. This provides both strategy and accountability in the use of God's money. The Southern Baptist Convention invites each local church to participate in a

larger kingdom enterprise by including the Cooperative Program as a line item in their budget.

Because of the autonomous nature of local churches, no dollar amount is specified. But in the early years many churches considered 10 percent to be a minimum gift to the Cooperative Program, as an example to the members of the church. Many churches also made a percentage contribution to the work of their local association, which assisted in larger Jerusalem-based projects.

Tragically, however, gifts forwarded from churches to the Cooperative Program have not kept pace in recent years with the increase in church offerings. "Churches have reduced their Cooperative Program giving from an average of 10.5 percent of their budget in the 1980's to 7.39 percent today. When the Cooperative Program was formed in 1925, the figure was about 11 percent."[13]

Theories abound as to the reason for the decline. I believe it begins with a failure to teach and embrace kingdom principles related to one's finances. Many churches were warned that visitors didn't want to hear about money. Actually, what they didn't want to hear were guilt-laden appeals to "meet the budget."

I have found that a balanced, biblical view of money, rather than being a turnoff or cause for offense, is an attractive and much-needed message. Our silence on this crucial topic has led to a reduced level of giving to the local church by the average member, which has in turn forced churches to retain a larger percentage for local operations. "Of the total inflation-adjusted dollar increases between 1968 and 2001, 93% was directed to congregational finances."[14]

This reduction of gifts to outside causes—to areas of need that exist beyond the walls of the church—has shrunk the average church's view of their role in the kingdom. That's why so many believers today are giving outside the local church. We have failed to share a convincing apologetic for how giving through the local church helps each of us fulfill the Acts 1:8 mandate. The resources are available, and our people want to give them, but we must give them a global vision.

2. *The state convention.* The first level of distribution of the Cooperative Program dollar is the state convention. The state treasurer has been authorized to reserve a set amount based on the vote of the messengers to the state convention. These funds are then retained to assist local churches in working together to accomplish goals at the state level—the Judea level—meeting needs that would be impossible to reach for any one church

working unaided. Percentages vary from state to state based on numerous factors. You can find the percentage allocated for your state's ministry by contacting your state office or getting a copy of the state budget.

3. *The Southern Baptist Convention.* Each state sends a check each month to the national convention through the Executive Committee for disbursement according to the Cooperative Program Allocation Budget, as approved by the messengers to the Southern Baptist Convention.

Since 1997 the SBC portion of the allocation has maintained a uniform percentage distribution among the entities. The International Mission Board allocation is 50 percent; the North American Mission Board's is 22.79 percent; the six Southern Baptist seminaries receive 21.64 percent; the Ethics and Religious Liberty Commission receives 1.49 percent; Guidestone Financial Resources receives 0.76 percent for ministerial relief; and the SBC Operating Budget Allocation is 3.32 percent.[15]

It's pretty impressive to notice that 94.43 percent of this budget goes directly to training ministers and supporting missionaries.

Yet I would suggest that *everything* in this budget is kingdom focused. The Ethics and Religious Liberty Commission helps Southern Baptists make an impact on issues of "salt and light" that impact the culture of our nation. Guidestone uses their entire budget allocation to assist ministers and their wives in retirement who are experiencing need. The Executive Committee works to inspire confidence in the denomination and to assist the entities in their work together. (If you're familiar with Southern Baptist life, you may be wondering what percentage goes to LifeWay Christian Resources and the Woman's Missionary Union. Actually, neither receives any funds from the Cooperative Program. They are both self-supporting.)

One of the reasons this pattern for the support of global missions has been so successful is that there is meticulous accountability at every level of allocation, disbursement, and reporting. Annual professional audits are preformed by every entity receiving Cooperative Program funds.

But the icing on the cake is this—*98 percent of every dollar given through this means is put to use in ministry.* That means administrative costs, including all accounting and promotion, consistently stay at around 2 percent.

The Cooperative Program stands apart because it is *not a budget for funding a denomination.* Instead, it is the *local church's budget,* enabling it to work effectively and efficiently with other churches of like conviction for the completion of the Great Commission.

The Premium Mutual Fund of Missions

Consider these benefits: A wide diversity of mission investments made with strategic intentionality. Trusted advisors with meticulous accountability. Low overhead. Excellent return on your investment. What else could you want in your mutual fund of missions?

You have no doubt surmised that I am Southern Baptist. I have written this section to provide a model for any reader from any denominational group, but it is only fair to tell you that I write as one who is committed to Southern Baptist life.

I have been privileged to serve as pastor of churches large and small. I have served the North American Mission Board, LifeWay Christian Resources, Southwestern Baptist Theological Seminary, and now the Executive Committee. My wife serves as a women's consultant for the International Mission Board. I have seen this denomination from nearly every conceivable vantage point, and I can tell you why I am committed to this mutual fund of missions approach.

- *I have confidence in our missiology*—that is, how we do missions. Our missiology defines *why* we cooperate. We cooperate because our King demands that we work with him to fulfill the Acts 1:8 challenge. We are privileged to have excellent strategists at our two mission agencies that constantly monitor our effectiveness in doing missions nationally and internationally. They are thinking strategically about how we allocate our mission forces for greatest kingdom penetration.
- *I am committed to our polity.* Polity defines our congregational governance. Our polity defines *how* we cooperate and allows us to ensure accountability at every level.
- *I am committed to our theology.* Theology affirms our focus and ensures that all resources are used to preach an authentic gospel and to plant biblical churches around the world.
- *I have confidence in our strategic plan.* We have in place partnerships at the local, state, and national levels that enable the local church to maximize its mission effectiveness.
- *I love a system that demands kingdom thinking.* All too often we give our tithes and offerings in such a manner that we can get credit for our giving or that we can control it. Kingdom giving requires that we reach out to people we may never see in person but who are still within our reach because of connections we've made with other brothers and sisters in Christ around the world.

There are trends today for a more direct missions' involvement. People and churches are taking mission trips around the world. I think this is a healthy trend. It gives people a personal view of what God is doing around the world and often stimulates them toward total mission involvement.

We must be careful, though, not to allow this to supplant the cooperative strategy we have in place. Those mission trips would have little long-term impact and would lack strategic purpose and continuity if not for our mission forces on the field. Therefore this trend, if not coupled with an overarching plan, has the potential of degenerating into a thinly disguised "societal method of doing and funding missions."

Kingdom commitment demands that we recognize our privilege and responsibility to use the resources in our stewardship wisely and strategically. It demands that we choose a lifestyle that will enable us to provide unusual resources for kingdom advance through our local church. It means that every local church should provide adequate resources for all four quadrants of our mission concern. And it means we must pray for and expect exponential and not incremental increase in mission giving and involvement.

It means working together with kingdom focus.

Week 6, Day 4

Revealed by Fire

If anyone builds on the foundation with gold, silver, costly stones,
wood, hay, or straw, each one's work will become obvious,
for the day will disclose it, because it will be revealed by fire;
the fire will test the quality of each one's work.
1 CORINTHIANS 3:12–13

A promising young architect and builder returned to his hometown to set up his business, quickly becoming famous for his unique designs and quality construction. Work poured in from all the surrounding areas as his reputation and business grew in equal portions.

One day the young man looked up from his desk to see the wealthiest man of the area standing before him. This man with virtually unlimited resources invited the young man to build a home for him, giving the architect *carte blanche*. He could design and build with no restraints. The specifications, location, and building materials were left entirely in the hands of the young builder.

So he began to design and order materials with absolute glee. He acquired beautiful and expensive wood and stone materials from around the world. No expense was spared.

But once the lot was chosen and the building project began, the young man's heart slowly began to change from a sense of gratitude at having been chosen for the task to one of resentment for having to build a "dream house" for a man too old to enjoy it.

He began to cut corners but only where it would never be seen. He used inferior quality materials for the foundation and the inner support beams. After all, no one would ever know. He knew the old man would die before the lack of interior quality was ever detected. The beautiful exterior would fool any unqualified onlookers.

But the old gentleman kept his promise and let the young man build unhindered, paying for anything and everything the young man ordered.

Finally the day came for the homeowner to take possession of his "dream home." But when the young builder handed him the keys, the old man turned his hand over and placed the keys in the hands of the young builder. "Son, this is your home. I wanted to give you the resources to build the home of your dreams. Enjoy it!" The young architect was both stunned and grieved. He knew the home would not last because the foundation was compromised.

My dad often used this story as a parable for the Christian life. And though I don't think I've told it as well as my father did, I have never forgotten it. Its truths and implications remain equally in force today. God has provided all the resources we could ever need for an abundant and effective Christian life, yet many of us build with inferior quality materials.

Paul used a similar story to challenge the Corinthians to live in such a manner that their lives would have a lasting impact for the kingdom of God. And in looking at it again, I pray we'll sense the Spirit's call to do something more with the much we've been given.

Building Is Not Optional

Many of the Corinthian believers considered themselves to be spiritual, but their behavior demonstrated the opposite. Paul addressed them as spiritual "babies" rather than mature believers. Their immaturity was demonstrated by childish disputes over spiritual leaders like Paul and Apollos. Their pride in being associated with certain men demonstrated a lack of understanding about the nature of the church and the kingdom.

Paul used himself and Apollos as examples of men who had been "graced" by God to be builders in his kingdom. He asked, "Who is Apollos? And who is Paul?" and then answered with the simple word "servants."

To be a servant is the way of the cross, the paradigm of ministry, and the only valid model for kingdom activity.

If you look at the full context of this passage, you will notice that the focus is always on God. Paul and Apollos each had the role "the Lord has given" (1 Cor. 3:5). Through their different activities, it was "God who gives the growth" (v. 7). They were privileged to be "God's co-workers" (v. 9).

And this is why Paul's primary concern was not himself. For both he and Apollos, the ones they cared about the most in Corinth were the Corinthians, not themselves as the church leaders. But the believers there had a hard time applying this in their own lives. In all their "spiritual posturing," they had ignored a fundamental truth: "You are God's field, God's building" (v. 9). The fundamental issue is ownership. God is the owner! The Corinthians were therefore God's possession, the same way Paul and Apollos were.

You can see it so clearly here—Paul shifting the focus from himself and Apollos to the Corinthians. The paragraph is dominated by words like "the one," "each one," "no one," and "anyone"—always talking about others, being concerned with other's welfare.

Paul was trying to say that rather than arguing about the leadership qualities of Paul and Apollos, the church should be focusing on the issue of their own response to the grace God had given them. No Christian can choose whether they intend to build with their life and resources. This is a nonnegotiable of the Christian life. I have never met a true athlete who wanted to sit on the bench. Athletes join the team so they can play in the game. Christians are chosen by God and gifted by his Spirit to build the kingdom!

So "each one must be careful how he builds on it" (v. 10).

This theme of accountability was already anticipated in verse 8 when Paul declared, "Each will receive his own reward according to his own labor." It is always safer to debate the contribution of someone else's life to the kingdom of God than it is to look carefully at one's own life. But in the final analysis, each of us will be held accountable for the grace resources we have received. The bottom line of our accountability is that we are building on a foundation that has already been laid, and thus the "stuff" of our life must match the quality of the foundation.

We don't like the idea of accountability—at *any* level. We rebel against it and often shout "unfair." While president of Southwestern Seminary, I often encountered students who argued that school would be enjoyable if it weren't for the papers, exams, and grades. They insisted that they would study just as hard and learn just as much if we dispensed with these kinds of imposing measures. I knew better.

While in college, I was allowed to take one course on a "pass/fail" basis. I intended to give this course the same attention I gave the others, but in truth I didn't. When push came to shove, I studied harder for the courses where I would be graded. I did just enough in my pass/fail class to get by.

Accountability is in the fabric of life itself. It adds value to life. If anything is worth doing, it is worth doing well. To use a secular analogy, it gives us a way to keep score. It assists us in knowing what value our life has and the contribution we have made.

So don't miss the exciting and affirming point of accountability. Your life does matter! You are "God's building!" He has created you with unique intentionality, and your life and resources count for the kingdom. God believes in you so much that he has chosen to allow you to build on the foundation established by his own Son.

Build well. And build often.

The Building Materials Are Your Choice

While building is not an option for the believer, we do exercise some control over the materials with which we build. "If anyone builds on the foundation with gold, silver, costly stones, wood, hay, or straw . . ." (v. 12). At first glance we can easily detect that there exists here a descending scale of value. The first three are more priceless than the final three. Further, in terms of building materials, the first three would be of higher quality and greater permanence. This is obviously significant in light of the fact that all of our building will be tested by fire, revealing the quality of our work.

The terms "gold, silver, costly stones" would have brought to mind the building of the temple. These terms are used in various combinations in the Old Testament to describe the building materials used in this great house of worship. When David invited the assembly to make contributions for the building of the temple, he first reminded them that the temple was for the Lord God. Then he told them what he planned to give—"To the best of my ability I've made provision for the house of my God; gold for gold articles, silver for the silver . . . as well as onyx, stones for mounting, antimony, stones of various colors, all kinds of precious stones, and a great quantity of marble" (1 Chron. 29:2).

If Old Testament man felt inspired to give in a sacrificial manner for the building of a physical temple, what then should we who are under grace be willing to give to build in the context of a kingdom that cannot be shaken (Heb. 12:28). This is truly the ultimate question of life!

We were created by God for his kingdom. We come into that kingdom through a relationship with his one and only Son (John 3). And therefore as kingdom children, our life's purpose is to advance his kingdom, by his power, for his glory.

But here is the point you may have missed when thinking about the question of what the kingdom person should use for building materials: *all the materials belong to the King, and he is willing to provide generously.*

Like the story of the young builder, we have a Benefactor who has given us an unlimited budget for building. I truly believe that if this truth gets beyond your head and into your heart, it will change you forever. You won't be clinging to "my money" or "my time" or "my talents." You won't be living life and giving of yourself like everything is about to "run out." His resources are inexhaustible, and he wants to make them available to those who will invest them in building his kingdom.

You are giving "gold, silver, costly stones" when you write your tithe and offering checks first, when you place opportunities for service before your own comfort.

But you are giving wood, hay, and straw when you worry about meeting your own needs before you offer your tithes and offerings to the Lord, when you promise God you will get more involved in ministry when you finish college, when the kids are older, when you retire.

Wood, hay, and straw or gold, silver, and precious stones—the choice is yours, but the consequences are certain.

The Day of Reckoning

Everything in life teaches us that there is ultimately a day of reckoning. We use a phrase like "pay the piper" to indicate that everything has its price, and one day that price will be paid. We overindulge during the holidays, and we pay the price when we return to the gym. We overspend at a big sale, and then the credit card bill brings us back to earth as we realize we'll have to make tough decisions to repay our debt.

The phrase "each man's work will become obvious" causes me to shudder. I remember times growing up when I would be in a hurry to finish a task assigned to me. I thought I could do shoddy work and fool my parents. It never worked. They always could see the quality of my work.

It causes me pause to realize that God not only sees the quality of my work, but on the Day of Judgment the quality of my work will be obvious to everyone. It is not that God wants to embarrass us, any more than an earthly parent would want to embarrass his child. It is simply that the quality of our work "will be revealed by fire" (v. 13).

Fire is associated with judgment throughout the literature of Judaism. Fire can both purify, as it does in the smelting of metals, or it can test the quality of something, as it does when it burns away the chaff. In this context Paul is clearly talking about testing the quality of one's life's work. As the day or dawn brings everything to light, so the day of reckoning will disclose every man's work.

This passage has nothing to do with losing one's salvation, as Paul makes abundantly clear in verse 15. It does, however, have everything to do with wasting a life that has vast potential for the kingdom. The phrase—"If anyone's work is burned up, it will be lost"—is a somber reminder that one day we will be held accountable for all the opportunities and resources God has given us.

I remember watching a young athlete in Galax, Virginia, squander incredible talent. I was grieved as I thought about his great potential that would never be realized. I am sure that God must likewise be grieved when he sees his children squander kingdom opportunities and kingdom resources. I don't know about you, but the idea of wasting a lifetime is a fate I want to avoid.

But we must also look at the flip side of this coin. "If anyone's work that he has built survives, he will receive a reward" (v. 14). Paul does not elaborate on the nature of the reward. It is certainly the reward of a job well done— the sense of satisfaction that comes from knowing we have done our best. But I suspect that he may have had in mind the ultimate reward reserved for the kingdom-focused person—the affirmation of the King—"Well done, good and faithful slave! You were faithful over a few things; I will put you in charge of many things. Share your master's joy!" (Matt. 25:23).

The Reward—"Well Done!"

One of the most famous parables in the Bible is that of the talents found in Matthew 25:14–30. You know it well. The master left his estate in the hands of his servants while he went on a journey. Upon his return each servant was called to give an accounting for how he had used the master's money.

The slave with two and the slave with five talents had invested theirs, doubling them. But the slave with one talent had foolishly buried his in the ground, fearing he might lose it. Therefore, this fearful slave was cast out while the two wise stewards were rewarded with increased opportunity.

This parable complements what we have learned from our study of 1 Corinthians 3 and allows us to draw several inferences.

1. *Our lives have meaning and purpose.* There are no insignificant members in the body of Christ.
2. *Everything we have is infused with kingdom significance*—money, talents, time, and opportunities.
3. *We are responsible only for what we have been given.* Comparing our resources or our kingdom assignment with that of someone else is irrelevant and counterproductive.
4. *The fear of failure is the tool of the adversary* to keep us from investing our lives in the kingdom.
5. *God loves and values us so much that he will hold us accountable* for the use of the resources he has loaned us. The Father's affirmation is enough.

My dad has been dead for several years now, but I can still remember the joy I felt when he placed his hand on my shoulder and indicated that he was pleased with me. No medal or earthly reward could compare with my father's simple affirmation. I can only imagine what it will be like to hear our heavenly Father affirm us for a life well lived.

Invest your life where it will make an impact for the kingdom. Refuse to bury your life and talents. God has created you for kingdom success!

Week 6, Day 5

A Kingdom Celebration

Therefore, since we are receiving a kingdom that cannot be shaken, let us hold on to grace. By it, we may serve God acceptably, with reverence and awe.

HEBREWS 12:28

I enjoy playing and watching golf, and I am a fan of Tiger Woods. His prodigious drives and ability to create shots has made him enjoyable to watch.

If you follow golf, you may be aware that Tiger recently suffered what some called a "Tiger Slump." He failed to win a major championship for an entire season, and he wasn't always atop the leader board. Tiger explained that he was redesigning his swing and that he was pleased with the progress. As you can imagine, everyone had an opinion.

Tiger silenced many skeptics when he won the Masters in 2005. Yet a few diehards pointed out that he bogeyed the last two holes to "hang on" for victory. The next big test came at the British Open, played at Saint Andrews. He entered the final round with a substantial lead, and it looked like all was well in "Tigerville." But on Sunday there was a moment when it appeared the momentum might be switching. Tiger made a bogey while Colin Montgomerie made birdie. These two events were on different holes but occurred at a similar moment. The anxious tension quickly passed, however, as Tiger birdied the next hole and went on to win by five strokes.

I didn't watch the tournament in real time since it was broadcast while I was preaching. By the time I was eating lunch, there was only one hole remaining to be played, and it was virtually a coronation event.

But when I arrived at the hotel later in the day, my wife—who had been at another church that morning—excitedly reported that there was a recap of the tournament we could watch together. I neglected to tell her that I knew who had won. She knows I'm a Tiger fan, and so when it appeared there might be a momentum shift, she looked to see how I was holding up.

I get involved when I watch sports on television. I saw her anxiously glance my way and told her to relax. "I bet Tiger birdies the next hole," I predicted with amazing accuracy.

It is stunning how accurate you can be when you have already seen the end of the tournament. It is also amazing how relaxed you are while watching the ups and downs of the drama when you know who ultimately wins.

I have some great news—the King wins, and his kingdom comes in glory. I have read the final chapter! And the knowledge of this ultimate outcome should inspire us to service, enabling us to keep the ups and downs of life in perspective.

Enthroned in the Heavenlies

When we look at the social and moral condition of the world today, it is sometimes difficult to believe that the kingdom of God is advancing toward ultimate victory. Marriages are in disarray; disobedience and rebellion are evidenced on every hand. Sexual immorality, drug abuse, and violence seem to rule the day from public schools to boardrooms. The war on terrorism has redefined our understanding of the phrase "wars and rumors of wars." The advance of Islam and the proliferation of cults have often made Christianity look anything but victorious.

Beyond that, we are confused by the general apathy of the Christian community. While we see pockets of church growth, some studies indicate that nearly 80 percent of churches in North America are either plateaued or declining. Most churches spend an inordinate amount of their resources on "keeping the doors open," while others seem obsessed on chasing the latest fad to attract and entertain its own members.

This is all set on a global stage where missiologists tell us 1.65 billion people have "little or no access" to the gospel. There are those who question whether the church in North America can be a viable player in the global advance of God's kingdom.

Yet in spite of all this, I promise you God's kingdom will be advanced to the ends of the earth and then the King will return in triumphant glory (Matt. 24:14).

The winning blow of the kingdom conflict was missed by many of those who viewed it in person. When the King's earthly life was destroyed by cruel crucifixion, many must have thought that the adversary had won. If you have seen the movie *The Lion, the Witch and the Wardrobe* based on C. S. Lewis's Chronicles of Narnia series, you have a good visual picture of the "defeat" that became the greatest victory of all time as Aslan gave his own life to redeem sinful man.

Jesus had told his disciples that the victory would be won in this seemingly unorthodox manner. "Now is the judgment of the world. Now the ruler of this world will be cast out. As for Me, if I am lifted up from the earth I will draw all people to Myself" (John 12:31–32). The resurrection was the conclusive declaration that the Son was victorious. He had entered the strong man's house and emerged triumphant. At that very moment the adversary's days were numbered.

Although he is a defeated foe, he is not yet banished from the earth, so he now resorts to deception and confusion to keep people from joining the advancing kingdom.

At this moment Christ rules and reigns from his royal position in the Father's presence. The sovereign Lord, the King of glory, is moving everything toward one final event—the judgment of the nations and the full and triumphant establishment of his kingdom. He orchestrates his work through his church, which is his full expression on earth. "He demonstrated this power in the Messiah by raising Him from the dead and seating Him at His right hand in the heavens. . . . And He put everything under His feet and appointed Him as head over everything for the church" (Eph. 1:20, 22).

Are you beginning to understand why Christ loves the church? Are you beginning to see what is at stake? Yes, I am talking about your church—the church you attend each Sunday. Your church is crucial to the work of the King until he returns. It can and must play a pivotal role in the reaching of your Jerusalem, Judea, Samaria, and the ends of the earth. You must think strategically in all these areas and learn to give of yourself and your material resources joyously and sacrificially to advance his kingdom until he comes.

God has created the world with resources sufficient for the advance of the gospel to the ends of the earth. And he has given a portion of those resources to you in stewardship, allowing you the privilege of participating in the greatest event in time and eternity—the coming of his kingdom.

It is indeed a grand joy and responsibility we share. And nothing compares with it!

Coming in Glory

The famous adage goes, "Only two things are certain—death and taxes!" But I promise you, one thing is more certain than that—the King is coming in glory. The early church lived in the daily anticipation and expectation of this. They would often use the greeting *Maranatha!* that means "Our Lord Come!" (cp. 1 Cor. 16:22).

Yes, he is coming! Can you see him? "One like the Son of Man, dressed in a long robe, and with a gold sash wrapped around His chest. His head and hair were white like wool—white as snow, His eyes like a fiery flame, His feet like fine bronze fired in a furnace, and His voice like the sound of cascading waters" (Rev. 1:13–15). We can almost make out the glorious features of his face as we imagine ourselves gathered in the throng that is comprised of "every creature in heaven, on earth, under the earth, on the sea, and everything in them" (Rev. 5:13), gathered to worship and adore the King of kings.

I, for one, do not want to miss that victory celebration. Beyond that, I do not want to show up empty-handed. I want to lay the gifts of ministry at his feet in loving adoration. I desire to celebrate with those who have joined this great company because of the investments I was privileged to make on Earth for the advancement of his kingdom. I want to live today in such a manner that the culmination of my life and ministry is this great kingdom victory celebration.

To Establish an Eternal Kingdom

God's heartbeat from creation to consummation is the liberation of planet Earth and the gathering of all peoples and nations at his throne to worship him as rightful King. Want to take a brief glimpse at the last chapter—at the coronation?

In Revelation 5 we have a scene too wonderful to describe in human language. The twenty-four elders are prostrate before the King. "And they sang a new song; 'You are worthy to take the scroll and to open its seals; because You were slaughtered, and You redeemed people for God by Your blood from every tribe and language and people and nation. You made them a kingdom and priests to our God, and they will reign on the earth'" (Rev. 5:9–10). The scene becomes even more glorious as John sees countless thousands plus thousands of angelic beings shouting with a loud voice, "The Lamb who was slaughtered is worthy to receive power and riches and wisdom and strength" (Rev. 5:12).

In Revelation 20 John sees the ultimate and final crushing of the "usurper king," the devil. This enemy is cast into the lake of fire and sulfur with the beast and the false prophet to be tormented day and night.

But John saves the best until last. He sees the new creation. A new heaven and a new earth! A new Jerusalem coming down out of heaven like a bride adorned for her husband. Those in this new kingdom—those whose names are written in the book of life—will never experience pain, death, or grief. But beyond all, they will know God in personal intimacy as a son knows his father.

While we revel in the personal intimacy of the moment, we must look at the bigger picture, the global picture.

At the end of chapter 21, John twice repeats that the nations will bring their glory into the new Jerusalem. "The nations will walk in its light, and the kings of the earth will bring their glory into it" (Rev. 21:24; cp. v. 26). The mention of the nations and their kings stresses the universality and preeminence of this city. The phrase "the glory and honor of the nations" (v. 26) does not imply that the nations add to the splendor of heaven, but rather that they lay everything at the feet of the rightful King. John envisions the salvation of a vast number from every nation. God's purposes will not be deterred, and his kingdom will come.

In Revelation 22, John described a "river of living water, sparkling like crystal, flowing from the throne of God and of the Lamb down the middle of the broad street of the city. On both sides of the river was the tree of life bearing 12 kinds of fruit, producing its fruit every month. The leaves of the tree are for healing the nations, and there will no longer be any curse. The throne of God and of the Lamb will be in the city, and His servants will serve Him" (Rev. 22:1–3a).

Are you getting the picture? God has a heartbeat, and his heartbeat is for all the peoples of all the nations to serve him.

Perhaps it escaped your attention in all of the celebration, but heaven will not be a place of indolent leisure where saints will sit in idle amusement for all of eternity. Heaven is a place where service abounds, all of it centering on God. If you haven't yet discovered the joy of praise and service here and now, this is fair warning—heaven is full of praise and service!

The Time Is Near

On three separate occasions in the last chapter, the resurrected Lord declared, "I am coming quickly!" (Rev. 22:7, 12, 20). In the first reference he assures the reader that "these words are faithful and true" (v. 6). Thus, the one who keeps or obeys these words is blessed.

The promise of a speedy return is repeated in verse 12, but this time the focus is on kingdom accountability. "Look! I am coming quickly, and My reward is with Me to repay each person according to what he has done." The word translated *reward* is literally *wages*. The idea that believers will be judged according to their works on earth is taught throughout the New Testament and is affirmed in this final warning. It would be tragic to waste a lifetime of kingdom opportunity and have no "wages" at his glorious return.

The final reference sounds the note of Christ's imminent return and is greeted with the fervent prayer that it will be so. "He who testifies about these things says, 'Yes, I am coming quickly.' Amen! Come. Lord Jesus!" (v. 20).

I have never been one to speculate about the time remaining until his glorious return, but I know one thing for certain—it is nearer now than it was the day John penned these words. Are you prepared for his return? Do you know for certain your name is written in the Lamb's Book of Life? If so, are you fully investing the Father's resources in his kingdom? Are your *wages* laid up in heaven?

If you are not satisfied with the level of your kingdom investment, why not decide to change that starting today?

It is beyond my comprehension that God would choose to use me to advance his kingdom and would personally provide all the resources in heaven and earth to enable me to participate in that task. I, for one, don't want to leave anything on the table. I want to invest fully in the kingdom of God.

Will you join me?

Appendix

If you have not yet entered a personal relationship with Jesus Christ, I encourage you to make this wonderful discovery today. I like to use the very simple acrostic—LIFE—to explain this, knowing that God wants you not only to inherit *eternal* life but also to experience *earthly* life to its fullest.

L = LOVE

It all begins with God's love. God created you in his image. This means you were created to live in relationship with him. *"For God loved the world in this way: He gave His One and Only Son, so that everyone who believes in Him will not perish but have eternal life"* (John 3:16).

But if God loves you and desires relationship with you, why do you feel so isolated from him?

I = ISOLATION

This isolation is created by our sin—our rebellion against God—that separates us from him and from others. *"For all have sinned and fall short of the glory of God"* (Rom. 3:23). *"For the wages of sin is death, but the gift of God is eternal life in Christ Jesus our Lord"* (Rom. 6:23).

You might wonder how you can overcome this isolation and have an intimate relationship with God.

F = FORGIVENESS

The only solution to man's isolation and separation from a holy God is forgiveness. *"For Christ also suffered for sins once for all, the righteous for the unrighteous, that he might bring you to God, after being put to death in the fleshly realm but made alive in the spiritual realm"* (1 Pet. 3:18).

The only way our relationship can be restored with God is through the forgiveness of our sins. Jesus Christ died on the cross for this very purpose.

E = Eternal Life

You can have full and abundant life in this present life . . . and eternal life when you die.

"But to all who did receive Him, He gave them the right to be children of God, to those who believe in His name" (John 1:12). *"A thief comes only to steal and to kill and to destroy. I have come that they may have life and have it in abundance"* (John 10:10).

Is there any reason you wouldn't like to have a personal relationship with God? It's as simple as ABC. All you have to do is:

- A = Admit you are a sinner. Turn from your sin and turn to God.
- B = Believe that Jesus died for your sins and rose from the dead
- C = Confess verbally and publicly your belief in Jesus Christ.

You can invite Jesus Christ to come into your life right now. Pray something like this:

> "God, I admit that I am a sinner. I believe that you sent Jesus, who died on the cross and rose from the dead, paying the penalty for my sins. I am asking that you forgive me of my sin, and I receive your gift of eternal life. It is in Jesus' name that I ask for this gift. Amen."

Signed _____

Date _____

If you have a friend or family member who is a Christian, tell them about your decision. Then find a church that teaches the Bible, and let them help you go deeper with Christ.

Notes

WEEK 1

1. *Enhanced Strong's Lexicon,* 7225.

2. Kenneth A. Mathews, The New American Commentary, *Genesis 1–11:16,* Vol. 1a (Nashville: Broadman & Holman, 1996), 23.

3. Derek Kidner, *Tyndale Old Testament Commentary, Genesis,* Vol. 1 (Downers Grove, IL: InterVarsity Press, 1967), 53.

4. Leo Garrett, "A Christian View of Material Things," *Resources Unlimited,* William Hendricks, ed. (Nashville: Stewardship Commission, 1972) 87–91.

5. Leo Green, "The Place of Material Things in the Purpose of God and the Life of Man" *Resources Unlimited,* William Hendricks, ed. (Nashville: Stewardship Commission, 1972), 70–71.

6. Ibid.

7. Kidner, *Tyndale Old Testament Commentary,* 68.

8. Fulton J. Sheen, *Footnotes in a Darkened Forest* (New York: Meredith Press, 1967), 121f.

WEEK 2

1. You might benefit from reading my book *The Prayer of Jesus* (Nashville: Broadman & Holman, 2001). If you would like to study the

material in a small group setting, there is a six-week study available at LifeWay Christian Stores or by calling 1-800-443-8032.

Week 3

1. Gerri Dertweiler, "How to Manage Your Money," radio program, Christian Financial Concepts, 24 March 1999.

2. Kregg Hood, *Escape the Debt Trap* (Fort Worth: Prime Source Providers, 2003), 5f.

3. Larry Burkett with Kay Moore, *Jesus on Money, Book 1: Charting a New Course* (Nashville: LifeWay, 2000). If you need further help with budgeting, you might find this six-week study particularly helpful.

4. Hood, *Escape the Debt Trap*, 6f.

5. Burkett, *Jesus on Money*, 80.

6. Hood, *Escape the Debt Trap*, 38.

7. John Murray, *The Epistle to the Romans* (Grand Rapids: Eerdmans, 1965), 159.

8. Hood, *Escape the Debt Trap*, 42.

9. Burkett, *Jesus on Money*, 62.

10. Robert Samuelson, "Hell No, We Won't Save," *Washington Post*, 17 February 1999, A17.

11. Burkett, *Jesus on Money*, 38.

Week 4

1. Oswald Chambers, *My Utmost for His Highest*, June 13 (Grand Rapids, Discovery House, 1992).

2. Epictetus, *Discources*, I, xvi. 20f.

3. If you would like to read about these festivals and others in Israel's life, you can read the article "Festivals" in *Holman Illustrated Bible Dictionary* (Nashville: Holman, 2003), 567–73.

4. R. T. France, *Matthew* (Grand Rapids: Eerdmans, 1985), 114.

5. "Giving Research," *Empty Tomb*, 16 December 2003, www.empty tomb.org.

6. Walter C. Kaiser, Jr., *Communicator's Commentary*, Vol. 21 (Dallas: Word, 1992), 472.

7. Joyce Baldwin, *Haggai, Zechariah, Malachi: An Old Testament Guide* (Sheffield: Sheffield Academic, 1987), 245–46.

8. Stephen Olford, *The Grace of Giving* (Grand Rapids: Zondervan, 1972), 29.

9. Ken Hemphill, *The Prayer of Jesus* (Nashville: Broadman & Holman, 2001), 65.

10. Ken Hemphill, *EKG: The Heartbeat of God* (Nashville: Broadman & Holman, 2004), 239.

11. France, *Matthew*, 138f.

WEEK 5

1. Stephen Olford, *The Grace of Giving* (Grand Rapids: Zondervan, 1972), 37.

2. Ibid., 40.

3. C. K. Barrett, *The Second Epistle to the Corinthians* (London: Adams & Charles Black, 1973), 219.

4. R. V. G. Tasker, *Tyndale New Testament Commentaries: 2 Corinthians* (London: Tyndale, 1969), 118.

5. John L. Ronsvalle and Sylvia Ronsvalle, *The State of Church Giving through 1992* (Champaign, IL: Empty Tomb, 1994).

6. Dean R. Hoge, Charles Zeck, Patrick McNamara, and Michael J. Donahue, *Money Matters* (Louisville: John Knox Press, 1996), 13.

7. Ibid., 15.

8. "Lifestyles," *Empty Tomb*, 3, www.emptytomb.org.

WEEK 6

1. Chad Owen Brand and David E. Hankins, *One Sacred Effort* (Nashville: Broadman & Holman, 2005), 62.

2. Robert A. Baker, *The Southern Baptist Convention and Its People, 1607–1972* (Nashville: Broadman Press, 1974), 97.

3. Ibid., 98.

4. Robert Baker and Paul Craven, *Adventure in Faith: The First 300 Years of the First Baptist Church of Charleston, S.C.* (Nashville: Broadman Press, 1982), 401.

5. Jesse C. Fletcher, *The Southern Baptist Convention: A Sesquicentennial History* (Nashville: Broadman Press, 1966), 114.

6. Brand and Hankins, *One Sacred Effort*, 88.

7. Baker, *Southern Baptist Convention*, 247.

8. *SBC Annual*, 1913, 316.

9. Catherine Allen, *A Century to Celebrate: History of the Woman's Missionary Union* (Birmingham: Woman's Missionary Union, 1987), 128–29.

10. C. E. Burts, "The Right Approach to the 1925 Program," *Baptist Courier*, 16 October 1924, 1.

11. Brand and Hankins, *One Sacred Effort*, 98. I have followed the outline of chapter 5 in this section and recommend the study of this excellent book.

12. Michael Foust, quoted in *Baptist Press*, 5 December 2005.

13. Ibid., 30.

14. "Giving Research," *Empty Tomb*, 16 December 2003, www.empty tomb.org.

15. Brand and Hankins, *One Sacred Effort*, 117.

Making Change
Workbook and Leader Kit

Multiply the message of *Making Change* across your entire church family with this interactive, small-group resource, complete with a companion guide to enhance discussion on the message of this book, as well as a DVD led by author and teacher Ken Hemphill, emphasizing the stories of what God has accomplished through the faithful giving of his people. Includes bonus planning and ministry resources for pastors and church leaders.

Call 1-800-458-2772 for more information on the *Making Change* workbook and leader kit, coming Spring 2007 from LifeWay Press.

More from Broadman & Holman Publishers

Look for these additional resources on Christian and church financial health from Broadman & Holman Publishers.

Wealth to Last
Larry Burkett and Ron Blue
0-8054-2785-6

Getting your Financial House in Order
David and Debbie Bragonier
0-8054-2720-1

Put Your Money Where Your Morals Are
Scott Fehrenbacher
0-8054-2449-0

Basic Accounting for Churches
Jack A. Henry
0-8054-6145-0

Basic Budgeting for Churches
Jack A. Henry
0-8054-6175-2